PRACTICAL TYPING EXERCISES Book One

Third Edition

Archie Drummond

Anne Coles-Mogford
Oxford and County Secretarial College

McGRAW-HILL BOOK COMPANY

London · New York · St Louis · San Francisco · Auckland · Bogotá · Guatemala
Hamburg · Lisbon · Madrid · Mexico · Montreal · New Delhi · Panama · Paris
San Juan · São Paulo · Singapore · Sydney · Tokyo · Toronto

Published by
McGRAW-HILL Book Company (UK) Limited
MAIDENHEAD · BERKSHIRE · ENGLAND

British Library Cataloguing in Publication Data
Drummond, A. M. (Archibald Manson)
Practical typing exercises.—3rd ed.
Bk. 1
1. Typewriting—Examinations, questions, etc.
I. Title II. Coles-Mogford, Anne
652.3'0076   Z49.2

ISBN 0-07-707040-2

Library of Congress Cataloging-in-Publication Data
Drummond, Archie.
Practical typing exercises, book one.
Includes index.
1. Typewriting—Problems, exercises, etc.
I. Coles-Mogford, Anne.   II. Title.
Z49.2.D78   1986   652.3'024   87-18092

ISBN 0-07-707040-2

Copyright © 1988 McGraw-Hill Book Company (UK) Limited.
All rights reserved. No part of this publication may be reproduced, stored in a retrieval system, or transmitted, in any form, or by any means, electronic, mechanical, photocopying, recording, or otherwise, without the prior permission of McGraw-Hill Book Company (UK) Limited.

1234 JWA 898

Typeset by
STYLESET LIMITED · Warminster · Wiltshire

Printed and bound in Great Britain by
J. W. Arrowsmith Limited

Preface

In any basic typing textbook, including our own Typing First Course, 5/E, it is not possible, because of lack of space, to give many examples of the exact layout of documents, or sufficient material for additional practice on the conventions of typewriting. Some students can become efficient typists by seeing and typing one or two model examples and a few undisplayed exercises, while other learners need more practice in typing from documents that are correctly laid out and easy to follow, and from less clearly displayed work.

In addition to being a fairly quick and accurate typist, the employer will prefer the junior typist who is:

(a) proficient in displaying business documents neatly and correctly;
(b) effective in following oral and written instruction;
(c) accomplished in comprehending and using modern business expressions;
(d) skilled in finding and using information from a variety of sources;
(e) capable of operating a word processor and electronic typewriter;
(f) able to make basic calculations.

With the foregoing points in mind, we have included in Practical Typing Exercises, Book One, Third Edition, the following additional features:

(a) users of word processors, electronic typewriters and computers with word processing capabilities will find certain tasks that may be used as **input**;
(b) **text-editing** changes for a number of exercises — instructions are given on pages 74–75;
(c) modern business terminology;
(d) exercises in which students have to refer to another part of the text for information to complete an exercise (names and addresses or extracting data from tables and other material) or in which they have to use an appropriate reference book.

Where students have to choose suitable margins, we suggest they use the following as a guide:

A5 portrait	typing line 50 spaces	12 pitch 13–63	10 pitch 6–56
A4 and A5 landscape	typing line 60 spaces	12 pitch 22–82	10 pitch 12–72
	typing line 65 spaces	12 pitch 20–85	10 pitch 11–76
	typing line 70 spaces	12 pitch 18–88	10 pitch—not suitable
	memoranda	12 pitch 13–90	10 pitch 11–76

Where a salutation/complimentary close has to be supplied, the complimentary close will be **Yours faithfully** if the letter starts **Dear Sirs(s)**. In other cases: Dear Mrs/Mr, etc, will close with **Yours sincerely**.

Target Times are given as a guide for the average student and these should be modified to reflect the overall level reached by an individual and the type of machine being used; obviously, a capable student operating an electronic machine with automatic facilities will type more quickly than, say, a person using a manual machine.

Open punctuation and blocked display have been used in all the exercises from pages 1 to 49. As in Typing First Course, 5/E, the exercises are then displayed with either full or open punctuation, with indented or blocked style of display.

This book follows the order of presentation of new matter as given in Typing First Course, 5/E, and as an aid to current, and, we hope, future users of that basic text, the page numbers of the relevant section of Typing First Course are shown at the foot of the pages. We would like to emphasize that this book can be used simultaneously with other textbooks or on its own.

Once again we express our gratitude to our colleagues for their valuable help and advice.

Archie Drummond
Anne Coles-Mogford

Index

Abbreviations, 1, 16
full punctuation, 50
Accents, 33, 41, 53, 63
Addressing envelopes, 29, 50
Agenda, 27
Allocating space, 48, 49
Blocked paragraphs, 52
Brace, 34
Business letters:
  attention line, 58
  blocked:
    full punctuation, 51
    open punctuation, 9–13
    column display 31, 32
    manuscript, 29–32
    urgent, 13
  semi-blocked:
    full punctuation, 58
    open punctuation, 57
    column display, 59, 60
  circular letters, 38–40
  display in body:
    blocked:
      full punctuation, 31, 32, 51
    semi-blocked:
      enclosure, 58
      full punctuation, 59
      open punctuation, 60
    subject heading, 58
    form letters, 24
    personal, 8, 62
Carbon copies, 5, 30
Cellular phones, 32
Centring:
  blocked, 2, 3
  centred, 53
Circular letters, 39, 40
Claim form, 22
Confederation of British Industry, 15
Correction signs, 35–37
Credit cards, 52
Credit notes, 26
Decimals, 1
Display:
  blocked, 2, 3
  centred, 53
Double spacing:
  blocked, 5, 6
  indented, 54, 56
Double underline, 21
Enrolment form, 23
Enumerated items:
  arabic figures and letters, 27, 28, 30, 31
  roman numerals, 38
Envelope addressing, 29, 50
Figures and words, 15
Footnotes, 36, 37, 42
  tabulation, 41, 42, 45, 65
Form letters, 24
Forms:
  claim form, 22
  enrolment form, 23
Forms of address:
  full punctuation, 50
Fractions, 1
Full punctuation, 50
Fully-blocked business letters
  (see Business letters)
Hanging paragraphs, 52
Headings:
  main:
    blocked, 4
    centred, 54
  paragraph:
    blocked, 5, 6
    indented, 55
    shoulder, 7, 39, 56
    side, 47, 49
    sub:
      blocked, 4, 5
      centred, 54
Horizontal centring:
  blocked, 2, 3
  centred, 53

Indented paragraph headings, 55
Indented paragraphs, 52
Information processing, 6
Information sheet, 76
Inset matter, 28, 30
Insurance details, 7
Integrated production typing project, 66–71
International paper sizes, 15
Invoices, 25
Leader dots, 60
  tabulation, 43, 46, 65
Longhand abbreviations, 16
Main headings:
  blocked, 4
  centred, 54, 55
Manuscript, 14, 15, 16
Measurements, 1, 15
Meetings, 5
Memoranda:
  A5 blocked, 17
  A4, 61
Minutes, 27
Money, sums of:
  in columns, 21
  in context, 1
Names and addresses, 9
Offset lithography, 36
Paragraph headings:
  blocked, 5, 6
  indented, 55
Paragraphs:
  blocked, 52
  hanging, 52
  indented, 52
Personal letters:
  blocked, 8
  indented, 62
Proofreading, 14, 72–73
  key, 74
Proofreaders' marks, 35
Punctuation (full), 50
Roman numerals:
  enumerations, 38
Ruled tabulation, 44–46
Secretary, The, 4
Semi-blocked business letters
  (see Business letters)
Shoulder headings, 7, 39, 56
Side headings, 47, 49
Sloping fractions, 1
Standard margins, Preface
Subheadings:
  blocked, 4, 5
  centred, 54
Sums of money:
  in columns, 21
  in context, 1
Superscripts/subscripts, 33
Tabulation:
  blocked, 18
  centred, 63, 64
  column headings, 20
  footnotes, 41, 42, 45, 65
  leader dots, 43, 46, 65
  ruling, 44, 45, 46
Telemessages, 16
Text-editing instructions, 74–75
Total (double underline), 21
Vertical centring:
  blocked display, 2, 3
  centred display, 53
Wages and salaries, 16
West Indies, 35
Words and figures, 15
Word processors, 28

FRACTIONS, DECIMALS AND SUMS OF MONEY IN CONTEXT

1. **Target Time: 7 minutes**

Type the following exercise on A5 landscape paper. Margins: 12 pitch 22-82, 10 pitch 12-72.

The washing machine is 820 mm high, 600 mm wide and 550 mm deep, and the maximum washing load is 4.5 kg (10 lb).

Everything for the well-organized individual in one smart 7¼ in x 5⅞ in x 1½ in leather ring binder.

The oven has a capacity of 54 litres (1.9 cu ft), and is 560 - 570 mm wide.

2. **Target Time: 5 minutes**

Type the following exercise on A5 landscape paper in single spacing. Margins: 12 pitch 22-82, 10 pitch 12-72.

The small table measures 2 3/10 ft x 1 2/5 ft - height 2⅞ ft, and should fit into the space available.

The machine washable slippers are in 67% polyester, and 33% cotton, in sizes 4, 4½, 5, 5½, 6 and 6½.

The camera bag is large and has everything for your needs, in size 9 5/8 in x 7 3/10 in x 6⅞ in.

3. **Target Time: 8 minutes**

Type the following exercise on A5 portrait paper in double spacing. Margins: 12 pitch 13-63, 10 pitch 6-56.

We are offering our casserole for just £21.25.

It was £28.30. Save £7.05 and pay in easy

instalments. You will be sent a statement every

28 days showing the amount you need to pay.

(The minimum charge is £4.00 per month.) There

is a small service charge of 2¼p in the pound,

that is 2.25%.

For an explanation of fractions, decimals and sums of money in context, see TYPING FIRST COURSE, 5/E, page 41.

INFORMATION NEEDED FOR VARIOUS EXERCISES

SPONSORED RUN AND BARBEQUE

DISTRIBUTION

Brownhill Centre	Nil
Spastics Society	£60.00
Youth Centre	Nil
Day Centre for the Elderly	£50.00
Elm's Children's Home	£120.00

KITCHEN EQUIPMENT

Item No.	Price
D70	£200.00
D82	£31.00
D151	£32.00
D172	£75.83
D191	£90.79
D521	£73.28
D600	£26.76
D622	£24.92

GENERAL OFFICE PRODUCTS

Stock Code	Price
1217	£14.77
1283	£2.22
2174	£75.50
2875	£8.20
2896	£9.60
2898	£83.99
2900	£3.20
3021	£2.80

McGRAW-HILL BOOK COMPANY (UK) LIMITED

Business Education Books

	Price
The Conference	£19.95
The World of Hotel Work	TBA
Numeracy Skills in Practice	£3.95
The World of Work	£5.95
Computer Literacy Skills	£5.95
Numeracy and Accounting	£6.50
The Practical Secretary	TBA
Know What I Mean?	£6.95
The Receptionist Today	TBA

TYPIST: There are often more items in a table than you require. Use only the information necessary to complete a document.

CONNECTING TRAINS FOR

Holyhead to Dublin*

	Morning	Night
London (Euston)	1000	2200
Wolverhampton	1125	2225
Birmingham	1110	2200
Bradford	1045	2031
Leeds	1022	1957
Coventry	1045	2200
Bristol	1030	1922
Manchester	1129	2235
Preston	1052	2130

* Subject to change without notice

STANDARD PARAGRAPHS (with code numbers)

Note to typist: You may wish to key in and store these sentences. You can then recall them as and when required.

-Sp1- If you have any more changes you would like to make, or discuss, please give me a ring.

-Sp2- Please tell us if you require further information.

-Sp3- I hope we can be of further service to you in the near future.

-Sp4- If you have any queries, please do not hesitate to get in touch with me.

-Sp5- If you require any items that are not listed, please do not hesitate to contact me.

-Sp6- Our experts will be pleased to visit your office to discuss your special requirements.

-Sp7- Full details are given on the enclosed pamphlets, and we look forward to hearing from you.

-Sp9- Please telephone us if you require further information.

-Sp10- Our order form is enclosed and we look forward to hearing from you.

-Sp11- If you are interested in participating in this promotion, details of which we enclose, we are able to offer a considerable subsidy. We should require 'before' and 'after' photographs, and a letter expressing your views on the process.

LEE, CLARK AND CRADDOCK

Price-List

Twin-deck Hi-Fi	£259.99
Compact Disc Midi	£430.00
Stereo Cassette	£129.99
Computer	£149.99
Remote Control TV	£299.99
Word Processor	£570.00
Portable TV	£179.99

THE PRACTICAL SECRETARY by Holmes and Whitehead

This text adds a new prospective to secretarial training, and, at the same time provides a clear, comprehensive and practical guide for all those who may have to carry out secretarial duties. Please order inspection copies by completing the attached order form.

HORIZONTAL AND VERTICAL DISPLAY

4. **Target Time: 5 minutes**

Display the following notice on A5 portrait paper. Centre the longest line horizontally and the whole notice vertically.

```
          N A T I O N A L     P A R K S

          in

          ENGLAND AND WALES


          Lake District
          Snowdonia
          Pembrokeshire Coast
          Exmoor
          Dartmoor
          Brecon Beacons
          Peak District
          North Yorkshire Moors
          Northumberland
```

5. **Target Time: 6 minutes**

Display the following notice on A5 landscape paper. Centre the longest line horizontally and the whole notice vertically.

T Y P I N G   C O U R S E S

DAY OR EVENING

Hours: 9.00-11.00; 1.30-3.30; 6.00-8.00

£1.10 per hour

Individual or Group Teaching
Keyboard Skills for Computer Operators
Word Processing Facilities

- EXAMINATION CENTRE -

If you have access to a word processor, an electronic typewriter, or a computer with a word processing programme, you may wish to follow the additional instructions given against the following symbol

When typing the above exercises, embolden the words typed in spaced capitals, use the automatic underline feature for the words underlined and the automatic centring key.

For an explanation of horizontal and vertical display, see TYPING FIRST COURSE, 5/E, pages 43-46.

Page 54 — Exercise 91
Change to single spacing with double, before, between, and after numbered (lettered) items. Delete the words 'For those of you who like variety,' and start the sentence 'May we . . .' Proofread soft copy and, if necessary, correct. Print out.

Page 55 — Exercise 92
Transpose the paragraphs TAX FREE and A NATION OF SHAREHOLDERS. Leave six clear spaces between the paragraph ending '. . . to pay tax' and the one starting CURRENT PLAN. Justify right margin. Proofread soft copy and, if necessary, correct. Print out.

Page 57 — Exercise 94
Change letter to fully-blocked style. Second paragraph — delete 'they are simple to operate and very cost-effective' and insert 'a beginner has no difficulty in learning to operate this machine in a very short time'. Proofread and, if necessary, correct. Print out.

Page 58 — Exercise 95
Delete the ATTENTION line and address the letter to Mr A Adams with the salutation Dear Mr Adams. Second paragraph — insert the words 'price-list and 'before the word 'catalogue'. Paragraph starting 'Also,' delete the word 'specially'. Proofread soft copy and, if necessary, correct. Print out.

Page 59 — Exercise 96
Delete the underline. Change the words 'White Wood/Laminate' to 'White Wood/Laminate/Oak'. Combine paragraphs two and three. Delete subject heading AUTUMN SALE. Proofread soft copy and, if necessary, correct. Print out.

Page 65 — Exercise 106
Change the prices for 'Combined Washers/Dryers' to £56.50 £83.90 £99.99. Proofread soft copy and, if necessary, correct. Print out.

Page 67 — Document 1
First paragraph — change to 'We thank you for your letter in response to . . .'. After '. . . centralized system.' type 'We can now arrange for your typist working at home to be linked to a dictating machine in your office by way of a public or private exchange line and the completed work can then be sent to you.' Second paragraph — change 'Mark III' to 'Mark II'. Proofread soft copy and, if necessary, correct. Print out original and one carbon copy.

Page 70 — Document 5
First paragraph — after '. . . automatic features,' delete the comma and insert '(centring, decimal tabulation, underlining),'. Transpose the paragraph about 'Word Processing' with the paragraph about 'Facsimile Transceivers'. Proofread soft copy and, if necessary, correct. Print out.

HORIZONTAL AND VERTICAL DISPLAY

6.   **Target Time: 5 minutes**

Display the following notice on A5 landscape paper. Centre the longest line horizontally and the whole notice vertically.

```
         T Y P E S   O F   E M P L O Y E R


         Sole trader

         Partnership

         Public corporation

         PUBLIC AUTHORITY - local government
                          - central government

         LIMITED COMPANY - private limited company
                         - public limited company
```

7.   **Target Time: 6 minutes**

Display the following notice on A5 portrait paper. Centre the longest line horizontally and the whole notice vertically.

```
          A GREAT DAY OUT!


          Bring the family


          Free entry to museums
          Fun fair
          Discount shopping vouchers
          Superb restaurants
          Great theatres and shops

          Send for your -

          D I S C O U N T   V O U C H E R S

          Don't delay - apply today
```

 When typing the above exercises, embolden the words typed in spaced capitals, use the automatic underline feature for the words underlined and the automatic centring key.

For an explanation of horizontal and vertical display, see TYPING FIRST COURSE, 5/E, pages 43-46.

ANSWERS TO PROOFREADING

Page 72 — Exercise 1a
Carrington & Son; 4 Castle Street; LIVERPOOL L2 4SW; Col T Manleigh OBE: Radcliffe Buildings; BIRMINGHAM B3 2BW; Ms R Wilson-Brown BA; Sir Patrick MacIntosh; 1 Holly Grove.

Page 72 — Exercise 2(a)
Transom House; Newcastle-upon-Tyne NE1 1DE; N E W; 6.30 am to 11.00 pm; Groceries Bread Milk Sweets; Fast Food; CALL IN TO SEE US!

Page 73 — Exercise 3(a)
206 High Street; OX2 1BH; (Tel: Oxford 73541); 2 Garrick 3-drawer pine chests; 3' mattresses (this should have been the second item); Heartwood 3' Nevada pine frames £175.20; Underbed pine drawers; stool.

WORD PROCESSOR OPERATORS — TEXT-EDITING INSTRUCTIONS

Page 35 — Exercise 62
Type the subheading in spaced capitals. Second paragraph — transpose the whole of the sentence which starts 'Sugar is its most important crop . . .' to the beginning of the paragraph so that it comes before the sentence which starts 'The north coast of Jamaica . . .' Proofread soft copy and, if necessary, correct. Print out original only in 10 pitch.

Page 37 — Exercise 64
Second paragraph — change 'As an undergraduate' to 'During his University vacations'. Third paragraph — transpose Thomas Hardy and Bernard Shaw. Last paragraph — delete the word 'short'. Proofread soft copy and, if necessary, correct. Print out original only in 15 pitch.

Page 39 — Exercise 67
Recall from file. Transpose the section about QUALITY OF SERVICE with the section about INVESTMENT. Justify the right margin. Last paragraph — after word 'progress' insert 'at the end of our financial year'. Proofread soft copy and, if necessary, correct. Print out.

Page 40 — Exercise 68
Recall from file. Insert today's date and address to Mrs R Q Lucas (address on page 50). Mark the letter PERSONAL and address an envelope. Proofread soft copy and, if necessary, correct. Print out.

Page 42 — Exercise 71
Delete items: LS 137 and TS 185. Change the price of item PL 130 to £123.50. Type the column headings in capitals. Proofread soft copy and, if necessary, correct. Print out.

Page 46 — Exercise 78
Use automatic centring device to centre main and subheading. Centre column headings. Start the table with 2 January and continue in chronological order so that the last month is December. Proofread soft copy and, if necessary, correct. Print out.

Page 47 — Exercise 79
Centre the headings and indent the first paragraph. POSTURE CHAIR — after 'adjustment.' add 'Excellent value at a reasonable price.' Change the typing to single spacing. Proofread soft copy and, if necessary, correct. Print out one original and one carbon copy.

Page 48 — Exercise 80
Delete the section about HALF-PRICE STANDARD DAY RETURN. Change the lettered items (a) and (b) to small roman numerals. Proofread soft copy and, if necessary, correct. Print out.

Page 49 — Exercise 81
Block the paragraph starting 'You can' at left margin and leave the 2 inch space on the right-hand side. Address the letter to H Becket & Co Ltd (address on page 50) and complete salutation. Change margins to 12 pitch 20-85, 10 pitch 11-76. Proofread soft copy and, if necessary, correct. Print out.

Page 51 — Exercise 85
Add a centred subject heading in bold print LINKED SCREENS. Add another item AS/31 1250 × 1500 mm dark brown £149.30. Change to indented paragraphs. Proofread soft copy and, if necessary, correct. Print out.

Page 53 — Exercise 90
Remove the underline where used and type those words in bold typeface. Underline '900 Bedrooms and 9 Lifts'. Centre the longest line and block all other lines at left margin. Proofread soft copy and, if necessary, correct. Print out.

MAIN HEADINGS AND SUBHEADINGS

8.   **Target Time: 8 minutes**

Type the following exercise on A5 portrait paper in single spacing. Margins: 12 pitch 13-63, 10 pitch 6-56. If you do not have a **bold type** facility, it is usual to underline the word(s) instead.

```
          ELECTRONIC TYPEWRITERS AND WORD PROCESSORS

          Modern Terminology

          A great many different word processors and word
          processing systems are used in business offices
          and the terminology used varies with the system.
          BOLD TYPE, BOLDFACE, BOLD PRINT, EMBOLDEN all
          have the same meaning: certain words may be
          emphasized by being printed in darker typeface
          in the print-out (hard copy).

          Hard copy is the name given to the text when it
          is printed out on paper (print-out) as distinct
          from soft copy which is the name applied to the
          data displayed on the VDU screen.

          In a business situation, the hard copy is passed
          to the originator who edits and returns it to
          the typist so that amendments (text-editing
          changes) may be made before a further print-out.

          Many systems may not operate unless you give
          the document a filename (sometimes referred to
          as codename or indexname).
```

9.   **Target Time: 6 minutes**

Type the following exercise on A5 landscape paper in single spacing. Margins: 12 pitch 22-82, 10 pitch 12-72.

```
T Y P E W R I T I N G

Homework Assignments

Once you have completed the keyboard, under the supervision
of your teacher, it may be beneficial for you to practise on
your typewriter at home.

If you do not own a typewriter, you can still undertake a
certain amount of work.  You can prepare exercises by reading
them through; there are points of theory that you must know
and be able to apply without hesitation; exercises that you
type in class can be checked and read through at home.

If you spend some extra time working on your own, you will
become a fast and accurate typist.
```

For an explanation of main headings and subheadings, see TYPING FIRST COURSE, 5/E, page 48.

PROOFREADING

Exercise 3   **Proofreading Target: 5 minutes**
                                                   Typing Target: 6 minutes

The details given in the handwriting in exercise 3(b) are correct. There are 13 errors in the typewritten version in exercise 3(a). When you have noted the errors, type a corrected version, making sure that you proofread your own typed copy very thoroughly.

Exercise 3(a) — to be corrected

THE PINE CENTRE   20b High Street   Oxford   OX2 1BL
(Tel: Oxford 73451)

PRICE LIST

Quantity	Item	Price
3	Garrich 3 drawer pine chests	£270.00
2	Heartwood 3' Nevada pin frames	£172.50
2	3" mattresses	£138.00
4	Under bed pine draws	£144.75
1	Garrick pine dressing table with Stool	£235.25

Exercise 3(b) — correct copy

THE PINE CENTRE 206 High Street Oxford OX2 1BH
(Tel: Oxford 73541)

PRICE LIST

Quantity	Item	Price
2	Garrick 3-drawer pine chests	£270.00
2	Heartwood 3' Nevada pine frames	£175.20
2	3' mattresses	£138.00
4	Underbed pine drawers	£144.75
1	Garrick pine dressing table with stool	£235.25

(Trs/ — transpose the mattresses row with the line above)

Answers to proofreading exercises on page 74.

For further details about proofreading, see TYPING FIRST COURSE, 5/E, page 64.

PARAGRAPH HEADINGS AND TYPING IN DOUBLE SPACING

10.   **Target Time: 6 minutes**
Type the following exercise on A5 landscape paper in single spacing. Margins: 12 pitch 22-82, 10 pitch 12-72.

<u>M E E T I N G S</u>

<u>Some terms used</u>

<u>The Agenda</u> is a list of items to be discussed at a meeting, typed in the order in which they will be dealt with. The Agenda may also contain the notice of the meeting, which should include the date, time, and place of the meeting.

<u>The Minutes</u> are an official record of a meeting. As a rule a verbatim record is not required, except for motions and resolutions.

<u>Convening</u> the meeting is usually the secretary's responsibility. This entails contacting those members who are entitled to attend the meeting.

11.   **Target Time: 6 minutes**
Type the following exercise on A5 portrait paper in double spacing. Margins: 12 pitch 13-63, 10 pitch 6-56.

CARBON COPYING

<u>Advantages.</u> It is a relatively inexpensive method of producing copies which can be made at the same time as the original. It is not necessary to use any additional, expensive equipment in order to reproduce the copies.

<u>Disadvantages.</u> Only a limited number of copies can be reproduced from one typing, and it can be time-consuming when correcting errors.

Embolden the main headings and use the automatic underline feature when typing the underlined words in the above exercises.

For an explanation of paragraph headings and typing in double spacing, see TYPING FIRST COURSE, 5/E, page 49.

PROOFREADING

Exercise 1 Proofreading Target: 5 minutes
Typing Target: 7 minutes

The following addresses, given in exercise 1(a), have been typed from the information given below in exercise 1(b). Exercise 1(b) is accurate, but there are 11 typing errors in exercise 1(a). When you have noted the errors, type the addresses on DL envelopes. Proof-read your own typing very thoroughly with exercise 1(b).

Exercise 1(a) — to be corrected

Carrington & Sons   Mr & Mrs M Black   Col R Manley OBE
Queen Street   4 Castle Road   Above Bar Street
LONDON   LIVERPOOL   SOUTHAMPTON
EC4N 1TT   L2   4SW   SO1 0FG

T O Kaur Co Ltd   Mrs R Wilson-Browne BA   Sir Patrick Macintosh
Radclife Buildings   Greek Place   1 Holly Grove
BIRMINGHAM   LEEDS   GLASGOW
B3 2PW   LS1 5SX   G6 3PU

Exercise 1(b) — correct copy

Carrington & Son   Queen Street   LONDON   EC4N   1TT
Mr & Mrs M Black   4 Castle Street   LIVERPOOL   L2 4SW
Col T Manleigh OBE   Above Bar Street   SOUTHAMPTON   SO1   0FG
T O Kaur Co Ltd   Radcliffe Buildings   BIRMINGHAM   B3   2BW
Ms R Wilson-Brown BA   Greek Place   LEEDS   LS1 5SX
Sir Patrick MacIntosh   1 Holly Grove   GLASGOW   G6   3PU

Exercise 2 Proofreading Target: 4 minutes
Typing Target: 5 minutes

The details given in the handwriting in exercise 2(b) are correct. There are nine errors in the typewritten version in exercise 2(a). When you have noted the errors, type a corrected version, making sure you proofread your own typed copy very thoroughly.

Exercise 2(a) — to be corrected   **Exercise 2(b)** — correct copy

TRANSOM SELF-SERVICE
Transon House
Newcastle-upon Tyne NE1 IDE

NEW

SUPER SELF-SERVICE STORE

Open: 6.30 am to 10.00 pm

Grocries Sweets Bread Milk
Fast Food Greeting Cards etc

CALL IN AND SEE US.

Answers to proofreading exercises on page 74.

For further details about proofreading, see TYPING FIRST COURSE, 5/E, page 64.

PARAGRAPH HEADINGS AND TYPING IN DOUBLE SPACING

12. Target Time: 7 minutes

Type the following exercise on A5 portrait paper in double spacing. Margins: 12 pitch 13-63, 10 pitch 6-56.

```
     INLAND WATERWAYS

     Method of Transport


     INDUSTRIAL REVOLUTION  In the late 18th century

     6,000 miles of rivers and canals in Britain became

     vital links between the seaports and the mills and

     factory towns.  The roads were still poor at this

     time, and new canals were opened well into the

     19th century to take all the traffic, which had

     increased because of the advent of the Industrial

     Revolution.


     LEISURE PURSUITS  Eventually the railways took most

     of the traffic away from the canals, and today

     they are used mainly for leisure.
```

13. Target Time: 6 minutes

Type the following exercise on A5 landscape paper in single spacing. Margins: 12 pitch 22-82, 10 pitch 12-72.

```
  INFORMATION PROCESSING

  Electronic Mail.  Messages can be sent from one work-
  station to another when this system is used.

  Icon.  This is a symbol or a picture on the VDU that rep-
  resents a function that can be performed by the machine.

  Bar code.  A bar code consists of stripes of various
  thicknesses that can be read into a computer with a pen-
  shaped reader.  These bar codes can be seen, for example,
  on a number of grocery items.
```

 Embolden the main headings and use the automatic underline feature when typing the underlined words in the above exercises.

For an explanation of paragraph headings and typing in double spacing, see TYPING FIRST COURSE, 5/E, page 49.

CLAIM FORM P2430

Please read the conditions of your policy before completing the form.

Policy No: BUS/23Z/901876

Name of insured: KENKOTT SCOTIA PLC

Address: Byrnes Terrace Langside Glasgow

Postcode: G41 3DJ

Telephone number (where you can be reached between 9.0 am and 5.0 pm): 041-486 2907

Situation where loss, damage or injury occurred: Typing Pool Office

Date of loss, damage or injury: 18 Nov. 1988

Explain fully how the loss, damage or injury occurred:
Three dictating/transcribing machines stolen fr. office by an intruder whose entry & exit was through a window. Reported to Langside Police Station.

Details of article for which claim is made	Date purchased	Present replacement cost	Amount claimed
Three dictating/transcribing machines	4 April 1988	£597.00	£597.00

Signature of insured:

Date: 23 Nov. 88

SHOULDER HEADINGS

14. **Target Time: 12 minutes**
Type the following exercise on A4 paper in single spacing. Margins: 12 pitch 22-82, 10 pitch 12-72.

INSURANCE DETAILS

Safeguard your property

BUILDINGS

Your individual premium will be linked to the likelihood of loss but will be at a very competitive rate. The new rate is just 15p for each £100 insured, despite the considerable increase in claims. The minimum premium for buildings is £30.

CONTENTS

As claims on contents insurance are not evenly spread throughout the country, and some areas have many more claims than others, we have introduced rating areas based on post-codes. The premium rates are given on the attached sheet.

ALL RISKS

The items under this heading cover the risk of losing or damaging personal property. Again the rates are given on the attached sheet.

CLAIM FORMS

Please read the claims conditions of your policy before completing these forms, which should be returned, together with the appropriate estimate for repair or replacement, to your insurance adviser.

 Embolden the main and the shoulder headings, and use the automatic underline feature when typing the underlined words in the above exercise.

ELECTRONIC OFFICE EQUIPMENT

Typewriters

Our complete range of electronic typewriters incorporates all the features that you expect in (moden) machines; daisy-wheel printing, (ausomatic) features, memory, etc.

Daisywheels

Our daisywheels offer a wide choice of different typestyles and can be interchanged in seconds to suit your (particlar) requirements.

Word Processing

A screen extension to our standard electronic typewriter range (will) give you a complete text-editing system. Text phrase and documents are all stored in the memory (156K disk storage) and can be (racalled) to the screen for updating/editing before printing out the perfect text.

Facsimile Transceivers

Is your office tied down by wasted time and redundant telephone calls? We have the answer. Let us demonstrate our new (facimile) transceivers. These machines are not only faster and more (relaiable) than the telephone, but also offer a combination of high transmission speed, compact (conveneince) and real economy.

 Key in document 5 (filename COMP) for 10-pitch print-out. Use automatic underline feature where words are underlined, EXCEPT for shoulder headings which should be in all capitals but not underlined. Justify right margin. When you have completed this exercise, turn to page 75 and follow instructions for text editing.

PERSONAL BUSINESS LETTERS

15. Target Time: 6 minutes

Type the following personal business letter on plain A5 portrait paper in fully-blocked style with open punctuation. Margins: 12 pitch 13-63, 10 pitch 6-56.

Social Work Journal
Dolphin Buildings
WALLINGTON
Surrey
SM6 0DX

Today's date

Mrs Rachel Pilkington
15 Howard's Way
LEATHERHEAD
Surrey
KT22 8AN

Dear Rachel

You will probably already know that we are holding a Seminar on (insert next Thursday's date).

If you would like a free ticket, please let me know.

Yours sincerely

Arthur Trueman

16. Target Time: 6 minutes

Type the following letter on a sheet of plain A5 portrait paper. The letter is from Arthur Trueman to Mrs Rachel Pilkington; therefore, apart from tomorrow's date, follow layout and wording in the letter above as far as the salutation; then type the following.

Many thanks for your phone call. It was good to hear from you.

I am pleased that you will be able to attend the Seminar on (insert date).

This letter is to confirm that accommodation has been reserved for you at the Royal Hotel for (insert date of day before the Conference date).

Very best wishes.

Type the complimentary close and Arthur Trueman's name, as in the letter displayed in the exercise above.

For an explanation of personal business letters, see TYPING FIRST COURSE, 5/E, page 53.

EXTRACT FROM BALANCE SHEET

31 December 1987

	Notes	1987 £m	1986 £m
Fixed assets			
Property	14	570.9	599.4
Investments	16	23.1	28.1
		594.0	628.5
Current assets			
Stock	19	256.6	316.6
Loans & deposits (tr)	22	17.6	13.9
Debtors	20	315.2	357.5
Cash at bank & in hand		29.5	22.7
		618.9	710.7
Capital reserves			
Called up share capital	27	132.9	129.5
Share account	28	118.3	103.1
Reserves	28	48.8	242.1 (tr)
Profit & loss account	29	171.0	44.0
		471	518.7

BUSINESS LETTERS

Refer to this sheet for the names and addresses of the addressees, together with the references and dates, when typing the letters on pages 10-13. The addressees' names are given in alphabetical order. Select the correct name and address for the letter you are typing. Insert the correct complimentary close. If the salutation is personal, eg, Dear Mrs Aziz, the complimentary close will be Yours sincerely. If the salutation is impersonal, eg, Dear Sirs, the complimentary close will be Yours faithfully.

Mrs K Aziz   Ref   HJB/TR   Date   26 April 1988
147 Fyfield Street
SOUTHPORT
Merseyside
PR9 9YF

Dr A F Cherill   Ref   AC/June/4638
Holly Tree House
BINGLEY
West Yorkshire
BD16 2LW

URGENT

Flt Lt Richard G Clowes   Ref   PRK/WT   Date   28 April 1988
Granary Cottage
China Lane
MANCHESTER
M60 1JW

Mr T Elliott
TV Cable Co Ltd
20 Riverbank Road
RIPON
North Yorkshire   HG4 1QE

FOR THE ATTENTION OF MISS CHRISTINE HORNE

Fraser Mitchell and Partners   Ref   RAZ/PBT   Date   25 May 1988
Long Lane
HARROW
Middlesex
HA1 1YR

SPECIAL NOTE
You may wish to key in and store the names and addresses given above so that you can retrieve them as and when required.

For an explanation of business letters, see TYPING FIRST COURSE, 5/E, pages 59-61.

Document 2   **Production Target: 8 minutes**

To Beryl P——   From Tom Brooksbank

Ref TJB/PAIL

When the new machinery is installed next month, we wl. need misc. items of magnetic media storage boxes for housing microfiche & floppy disks. Access is important. As you perhaps already know, the disks are 5¼". & I feel th. we must carefully consider the boxes w. transparent lids.

Another point to bear in mind is that the storage boxes must be fireproof & suitable for lateral filing.

Document 3   **Production Target: 8 minutes**

TO: ALL MARKETING AND SALES STAFF

A meeting of marketing & sales staff wl be held in the Sales Manager's Office at 1030 hours on 18 Dec.

AGENDA ← (spaced caps)

1. Apologies
2. Sales figures for July, August, Sept.
3. Future marketing
4. New lines
5. (a) New representative for area 2
   (b) Change of address for area 3
6. Use of telephone
7. & Any other business

(Leave 1" clear here)

T J BROOKSBANK
MARKETING DIRECTOR

BUSINESS LETTER WITH ENCLOSURE

17.   **Target Time: 10 minutes**

Type the following fully-blocked letter in open punctuation, from Kenkott Scotia PLC, on A4 letterhead paper, which will be found in the HANDBOOK AND SOLUTIONS MANUAL, 5/E. Margins: 12 pitch 22-82, 10 pitch 12-72. The reference, date, and name and address of the addressee will be found on page 9 of this textbook. Insert a suitable complimentary close.

Dear Mrs Aziz

I am enclosing the revised plan and quotation, incorporating the amendments we discussed last week.

Item Number 12 is changed from a 400 mm wide base cupboard to a 300 mm wide base cupboard, thus enlarging the space available between the door and the cupboard.

You will note that I have included, in the new quotation, the removal of the radiator which stands, at the moment, against the low wall. A short length of one of the chopped off pipes may be visible.

Item 24 is a 300 mm wide wall cupboard. Unfortunately, this was omitted from the previous quotation.

If you have any more changes you would like to make, or discuss, please give me a ring.

Henry J Badcock
Design Department

Enc

For an explanation of business letters with enclosure, see TYPING FIRST COURSE, 5/E, pages 56 and 60.

Document 1 Production Target: 25 minutes

Our Ref TJB/market/D117

Paisley Office Supplies Ltd
12 Edinburgh Road
PAISLEY
Lanarkshire   PA2 7RG

DICTATING TRANSCRIBING MACHINES

We ack. receipt of yr. letter regarding our latest advert. in the Paisley Evening News. These dictating machines are available in 3 styles: portable & desk top. We wl also install a centralized system. The jewel among dictating machines is the Mark III wh. has the smallest recording cassette on the market. You can dictate for 40 mins. on ea. side & this is a feature th. few mini-cassettes offer.

The desk models hv. facilities like 'afterthought' – inserting an extra recording on a tape w'out disturbing existing dictation. Our reputation for reliability & commitment to research & development are bywords in the industry, & we look forward to hearing fr. you when you hv. studied the enclosed brochures.

Yrs ffy
KENKOTT SCOTIA PLC

T J BROOKSBANK MARKETING DIRECTOR

Key in document 1 (filename COMP) for 12-pitch print-out. Embolden the ATTENTION line and the subject heading. Use the automatic underline feature for the words underlined. When you have completed this exercise, turn to page 75 and follow instructions for text editing.

BUSINESS LETTERS WITH SUBJECT HEADING

18.   **Target Time: 6 minutes**

Type the following fully-blocked letter in open punctuation, from Kenkott Scotia PLC, on A5 letterhead paper. Margins: 12 pitch 13-63, 10 pitch 6-56. Insert the date: 1 July 1988; and the enclosure notation. The reference and name and address of the addressee will be found on page 9 of this textbook. Insert a suitable complimentary close.

```
Dear Dr Cherill

JUNE QUARTER 1988

I have pleasure in enclosing your statement of
account, together with a cheque for £68, in
respect of the overpayment made by you at the
beginning of June.

If you have any queries, please do not hesitate
to get in touch with me.




Anthea Cheung (Ms)
Finance Department

Encs
```

19.   **Target Time: 6 minutes**

Type the following letter from Kenkott Scotia PLC on A5 letterhead paper. Margins: 12 pitch 13-63, 10 pitch 6-56. Insert date: 4 July 1988. Follow the layout and wording in the letter above, apart from the date, as far as the first paragraph, then type the following.

```
I wish to apologize most sincerely for omitting
to enclose the cheque for £68 in my letter to
you of 1 July.

I do hope that this has not inconvenienced you
in any way, and I now enclose the cheque with
this letter.
```

Type the complimentary close and Ms Cheung's name as in exercise 18. As there is only one enclosure with this letter, type Enc not Encs.

For an explanation of business letters with subject headings, see TYPING FIRST COURSE, 5/E, pages 57 and 60.

KENKOTT SCOTIA PLC
TYPING POOL – REQUEST FORM

This sheet contains instructions which must be complied with when typing the documents. Read the information carefully before starting, and refer back to it frequently.

Typist's log sheet

Originator **T J BROOKSBANK** Department *Marketing* Date *23 Nov. '88* Ext No *2173*

 Typists operating a word processor, or electronic typewriter with appropriate function keys, should apply the following automatic facilities: top margin; carrier return; line-end hyphenation; underline OR bold print (embolden); error correction; centring; any other relevant applications.

Remember to (a) complete the details required at the bottom of the form; (b) enter typing time per document in appropriate column; and (c) before submitting this Log sheet and your completed work, enter TOTAL TYPING TIME in last column so that the typist's time may be charged to the originator.

Document No	Type of document and instructions	Copies – Original plus	Input form ¶	Typing time per document	Total typing time ¥
1	Letter to Paisley Office Supplies FOR THE ATTENTION OF MRS H FOWLER Insert salutation Please type an envelope	1 orig. + 1 carbon	MS		
*2	Memo to Beryl Phillips	1 orig. + 1 carbon	MS		
3	Notice of meeting Use A5 paper	1 orig. + 3 photocopies	MS		
4	Extract for Balance Sheet. Use headed paper.	1 orig.	MS		
5	Amended Typescript. Correct circled words	1 orig.	AT		
6	Details to be typed on blank claim form	1 orig.	MS		
				TOTAL TYPING TIME	

TYPIST – please complete:
Typist's name: Date received: Date completed:
                 Time received: Time completed:

If the typed documents cannot be returned within 24 hours, typing pool supervisor should inform the originator. Any item that is urgent should be marked with an asterisk (*).

¶ T = Typescript   AT = Amended Typescript   MS = Manuscript   SD = Shorthand Dictation   AD = Audio Dictation
¥ To be charged to the originator's department.

Integrated production typing project

BUSINESS LETTER — FOR THE ATTENTION OF

20.   **Target Time: 12 minutes**

Type the following letter from Kenkott Scotia PLC on A4 letterhead paper. Margins: 12 pitch 22-82, 10 pitch 12-72. The reference, date, and name and address of the addressee will be found on page 9 of this textbook. Mark the letter FOR THE ATTENTION OF MISS CHRISTINE HORNE. Insert a suitable complimentary close.

```
Dear Sirs

RANGE OF SUPPLIES

You will be pleased to know that, in order to be able to
offer you a complete service, we have recently extended our
range of supplies.

Among the additions to our range is a new miniwash with
built-in tumble drier.  It weighs only 21 lb, the washer
takes up to a 4.4 lb load, and the drier up to 2.2 lb of
clothes.  Details of this, and other products, are given in
the enclosed catalogue.

If you require any items that are not listed, please do not
hesitate to contact me.




R A ZIMMERMAN
Sales Support Manager

Enc
```

 Embolden the subject heading when typing the above exercise.

For an explanation of business letters with for the attention of, see TYPING FIRST COURSE, 5/E, page 58.

CENTRED RULED TABULATION WITH LEADER DOTS

106. **Target Time: 20 minutes**

Type the following table on A4 paper. Centre vertically and horizontally. Insert leader dots and rule.

HOUSEHOLD INSURANCE SCHEME

Climax Insurance Co Ltd

Appliance	2 years	4 years	5 years
	£	£	£
Combined Washers/Dryers	100.50	189.00	208.00
Dishwashers	16.50	41.50	63.50
Gas Cookers	14.00	30.00	42.50
Gas Fires	8.50	16.00	21.50
Fridges and Freezers* .	12.00	25.00	33.00
Hobs	9.50	23.50	31.50
Hoods	10.50	23.50	31.50
Twin-tub Washers	14.00	30.00	42.50
Vacuum Cleaners	8.50	16.00	22.50
Water Heaters	14.00	30.00	42.50

* Includes Food Spoilage up to £300.00

Key in the above document (filename INS) for 12-pitch print-out. Use bold type for main heading, the automatic underline feature for the subheading, and decimal tabs for the money columns. Utilize the save function for the first horizontal ruled line and copy it where necessary, and employ the vertical line key as appropriate. When you have completed this exercise, turn to page 75 and follow instructions for text editing.

For an explanation of centred tabulation with leader dots, see Typing First Course, 5/E, page 134.

FULLY-BLOCKED BUSINESS LETTER

21. Target Time: 12 minutes

Type the following letter from Kenkott Scotia PLC on A4 letterhead paper. Margins: 12 pitch 22-82, 10 pitch 12-72. The reference, date, and full name and address of Flt Lt Clowes will be found on page 9 of this textbook. Mark the letter URGENT. Insert a suitable complimentary close.

Dear Sir

SPRING CATALOGUE

It is certainly a pleasure to be sending you this Spring edition of our DIY catalogue. We are sure you will find it of great interest, with many useful items.

As you will see, there is an amazing variety of goods - tools, accessories, equipment and furniture - all carefully selected, checked and tested.

We offer prompt, first-class service. Just complete the order form at the back of the catalogue, and the goods will be delivered within 14 days.

If you are not entirely satisfied, please return them within 2 weeks, unused, and your money will be refunded in full.

Pat R Kelly (Mrs)
Marketing Manager

Enc

  Embolden the word URGENT and the subject heading when typing the above exercise.

CENTRED TABULATION WITH COLUMN HEADINGS — HORIZONTAL AND VERTICAL RULING

104. **Target Time: 15 minutes**

Type the following exercise on A5 landscape paper in double spacing. Centre the exercise vertically and horizontally and rule.

CAR COLOURS - DECEMBER 1987

SOLID	METALLIC	TWO-COAT
Ceramic Red	Fjord Blue	Carnelian Red
Jamaica Yellow	Olive Green	Dolphin Grey
Mexico Red	Sapphire Blue	Helios Blue
Nordic Blue	Silver Blue	Saxon Bronze
Polar White	Turquoise	Steel Grey

105. **Target Time: 15 minutes**

Type the following exercise on A5 portrait paper in double spacing. Centre the exercise horizontally and vertically and rule.

COLOURS AND TRIMS

Exterior Colours	Trims
Almadine Red	Beige
Black	Beige/Grey
Gazelle Beige	Brown
Monaco Blue)) Navy Blue)	Blue/Grey
Polar White	Grey
Saxon Bronze	Brown/Grey

For an explanation of centred tabulation with column headings, horizontal and vertical ruling, see TYPING FIRST COURSE, 5/E, page 166.

PROOFREADING — TYPING FROM MANUSCRIPT

22. **Target Time: 14 minutes**
Display the following exercise on A4 paper in double spacing. Margins: 12 pitch 22-82, 10 pitch 12-72.

PROOFREADING

Check for accuracy

CHECK FORMAT OR LAYOUT

Check the document to make sure there are no errors in display. For example, incorrect linespacing or the omission of a heading will mean that the document will need to be retyped.

READ THROUGH FOR ACCURACY OF CONTENT

If the document is read through carefully for content and meaning, it should be possible to find 'hidden errors', eg, words or even lines omitted. Ideally, it is preferable to ask the help of a colleague to read the original document through to you while you check the typescript. Omissions are then more easily spotted.

PROOFREAD FOR TYPOGRAPHICAL ERRORS

The document should be read through a third time for typographical errors which should be corrected neatly on both the top and any carbon copies.

 Embolden the main and shoulder headings, and use the automatic underline feature when typing the above exercise.

For an explanation of proofreading and typing from manuscript, see TYPING FIRST COURSE, 5/E, page 64.

CENTRED TABULATION — WITH AND WITHOUT COLUMN HEADINGS

101.   **Target Time: 8 minutes**

Type the following exercise on A5 landscape paper in double spacing. Centre the exercise vertically and horizontally.

P O S T A L   S E R V I C E S

⇐International Reply	⇐Advice of Delivery	⇐Aerogrammes
Letters	Cash on Delivery	Airmail
Newspapers	Datapost	Express Delivery
Periodicals	Parcel Post	*Intlepost*
Printed Papers	Small Packets	Swiftair

(Please check spelling)

102.   **Target Time: 10 minutes**

Type the following exercise on A5 portrait paper in double spacing. Centre the exercise vertically and horizontally.

W I N T E R   C R U I S E S

ENJOY THE WINTER SUNSHINE!

Place	Date	Number of Days
Madeira	16-27 December	12
Naples	17-28 Dec	12
Tenerife	1-14 Jan	14
Genoa	16-25 Jan	10
Istanbul	1-12 Feb	12
Freetown	15-21 Feb	7

103.   **Target Time: 10 minutes**

Type the following exercise on A5 landscape paper in double spacing. Centre the exercise vertically and horizontally.

YOUR ELECTRIC CASSEROLE

Slow Cooking made Simple   *uc*

SOUPS	MEAT AND OTHER DISHES	PUDDINGS
Celery	Beef Olives	Creamed Rice
Leek	Irish Stew	Ginger Sponge
Lentil	Liver Pâté	Jam Sponge
Potato	Soused Herrings	Marmalade

For an explanation of centred tabulation with and without column headings, see TYPING FIRST COURSE, 5/E, pages 164 and 165.

TYPING MEASUREMENTS — USE OF WORDS AND FIGURES

23. **Target Time: 8 minutes**

Type the following on A5 landscape paper in single spacing. Margins: 12 pitch 22-82, 10 pitch 12-72.

INTERNATIONAL PAPER SIZES

The adoption of the international A size of paper brings greater economy to users of paper.

A4 paper measures 210 mm x 297 mm (8.27 in x 11.69 in). Quarto paper, which was in general use before the adoption of the international sizes, measures 8 in x 10 in. A5 paper measures 148 mm x 210 mm (5.83 in x 8.27 in). This replaced octavo paper which measured 5 in x 8 in.

24. **Target Time: 10 minutes**

Type the following exercise on A5 portrait paper in single spacing. Margins: 12 pitch 13-63, 10 pitch 6-56.

THE CONFEDERATION OF BRITISH INDUSTRY

The Confederation of British Industry (CBI) was founded in August 1965, and is a non-party political body financed entirely by industry and commerce. The CBI represents more than 300,000 companies.

The governing body of the CBI is the 400-strong Council. It is assisted by some 30 expert standing committees which advise on the main aspects of policy. Thirteen Regional Councils and offices cover the administrative regions of England, Scotland, Wales and Northern Ireland.

For an explanation of typing measurements and use of words and figures, see TYPING FIRST COURSE, 5/E, page 70.

PERSONAL LETTERS WITH HOME ADDRESS CENTRED AND ALSO BLOCKED TO THE RIGHT

99. **Target Time: 7 minutes**

Type the following letter on plain A5 portrait paper. Margins: 12 pitch 13-63, 10 pitch 6-56. Centre the home address on the page. Use semi-blocked style and open punctuation.

```
              29 Frederick Road
                   EPSOM
              Surrey   KT19 8BE


                              29 July 1988

Focal Fireplaces Ltd
9 West Boulevard
EPSOM
Surrey   KT18 7HB

Dear Sirs

     Thank you for your quotation dated 25 July
for a gas log- and coal-effect fire.  I accept
your quotation for the sum of £262.85.

     Would you please arrange for your fitter to
install this fire on Monday, 8 August.

                    Yours faithfully



                    John R Mallon
```

100. **Target Time: 7 minutes**

Type the following letter on plain A5 portrait paper. Margins: 12 pitch 13-63, 10 pitch 6-56. Block the home address at the right margin. Use semi-blocked style and open punctuation.

```
                         10 Hillshaw Road
                                 RIPON
                        North Yorkshire
                               HG4 1AA

                              1 August 1988
```

Please address to Mr. I Elliott — address on page 9 — and insert salutation.

```
     Thank you for your quotation for fitting an
Intruder Alarm for the sum of £720 plus VAT.

     I look forward to your engineers starting on
the installation on Tuesday, 9 August.

                    Yours sincerely
```

For an explanation of semi-blocked personal letters with home address centred and also blocked to the right, see TYPING FIRST COURSE, 5/E, page 163.

LONGHAND ABBREVIATIONS

25.   Target Time: 7 minutes

Type the following exercise on A5 landscape paper in single spacing. Margins: 12 pitch 22-82, 10 pitch 12-72. Please check from your telephone directory to see whether or not the name and address is included free of charge. If not, change the wording accordingly.

TELEMESSAGES

The sec. can send a Telemessage at any time — the call is free — but if you wish the message to arrive the next working day, including Sat., the call must be made before 10 pm. Telemessages can be sent thro' the Telex network, or by telephone. Use the Telemessage service for urgent appts., or to book accom.

Yr. message is printed on A4 paper, & delivered in a bright yellow & blue envelope. Telemessages are charged for in blocks of 50 words. The name & address is included free of charge.

I recom. the Telemessage for social as well as business occasions; for weddings, birthdays, or some special event.

26.   Target Time: 7 minutes

Type the following exercise on A5 portrait paper in double spacing. Margins: 12 pitch 13-63, 10 pitch 6-56.

WAGES & SALARIES

<u>Gross Pay</u>   This is the total amt. earned by an employee. It is the basic pay, plus any additional payments. For example, if you are entitled to a bonus, this wl. be added to yr. gross pay.

<u>Net Pay</u>   The amt. wh. is actually recd. by an employee is known as net pay. The employer deducts certain items from yr. gross pay, eg, income tax & national insurance. The amt. wh. remains is the sum of money you wl. receive. Yr. pay slip wl. show you yr. gross pay, any deductions that have been made, & yr. net pay.

For an explanation of longhand abbreviations, see TYPING FIRST COURSE, 5/E, page 71.

98. Target Time: 15 minutes

Type the following exercise on A4 memo paper. Take one carbon copy.

To Jim Campbell
17 Oct '88

From Arthur Livingstone
AL/MH

IMPERIAL 5-DOOR HATCHBACK

A meeting of sales staff will be held in my office at 9am on Mon. 24 Oct. to discuss campaign for the sale of this new hatchback. The Imperial has a 2.0 engine & an outstanding blend of distinctive looks & features. Luxury, style, & performance are the keywords — all 3 qualities are very evident in the latest model. In our campaign we must concentrate on the following new features:

(a) 2.0 engine — perfect relaxation when travelling at high speed
(b) luxury cloth trim
(c) see-through front seat head restraints
(d) 5-speed overdrive gearbox
(e) sliding and tiltable glass sunroof w. interior sunblind
(f) adjustable & tiltable steering column
(g) rear seat belts.

We must not forget to emphasize the now standard aspects of previous models such as central locking, electrically operated windows, headlamp wash/wipe, etc.

(Typist — please inset the lettered items 6 spaces from left margin)

Please stress to sales staff the importance of this meeting. Only in exceptional circumstances wl I accept an excuse for absence.

MEMORANDA

27. Target Time: 6 minutes

Type the following memo on a printed A5 memo form, copies of which are in the HANDBOOK AND SOLUTIONS MANUAL, 5/E. Margins: 12 pitch 13-90, 10 pitch 11-76.

MEMORANDUM

From Carol McAllister, Finance Dept

To F Khimji, Personnel Dept

Date 25 July 1988

VENDING MACHINES

As you know, the staff canteen wl not be open during mid-morning or mid-afternoon, but only for lunches between the hrs of 1215 & 1400.

It has bn decided, therefore, to purchase 6 vending machines, one for each floor of the building. This wl enable staff to have coffee, tea and/or snacks during the mid-morning or mid-afternoon breaks.

The machines wl be installed next week.

C McA/PR

28. Target Time: 6 minutes

Type the following memo on a printed A5 memo form, copies of which are in the HANDBOOK AND SOLUTIONS MANUAL, 5/E. Margins: 12 pitch 13-90, 10 pitch 11-76.

MEMORANDUM

From William Stilgoe

To Trevor Almond

Date 28 July 1988

RADIO MOBILE PHONES

At the last mtg of the Board, it was decided to install radiophones in the cars used by our representatives. This wl enable them to make & receive calls while travelling to and from customers, with an obvious saving in time.

I shd be glad if you wld make arrangements to have the 8 cars belonging to the Co to be fitted with the automatic radiophone equipment.

I am enclosing a leaflet wh gives full details.

WT/BT

For an explanation of memoranda, see TYPING FIRST COURSE, 5/E, page 76.

SEMI-BLOCKED LETTER WITH DISPLAYED MATTER

97. Target Time: **14 minutes**

Using headed paper, type the following letter from Eastways Developments (UK) Ltd in semi-blocked style with open punctuation. Take a carbon copy and centre the subject heading and displayed portion. Insert leader dots where shown and correct words that are circled.

Our Ref AK/PAC/Disk 3/399   21 Sept. 1988

Your Ref GA/SR/WP 9/32

FOR THE ATTENTION OF MR W GROVES

Messrs P Callow & Sons
17 Newport Way
MONMOUTH
Gwent
NP5 3TS

Dear Sirs

AUTOMATED FILING SYSTEMS

Thank you for yr letter dated 19 Sept. asking us to send you details of our electronic fileing system.

Our classic range of filing cabinets is a compact & reliable filing system capable of storing up to 60,000 A4 docs.

The attached data sheets explain the system in detail; however, there is one or 2 points we would like to make.

The environmental conditions required are as follows:

    Operational Temperature   10-32 °C
    Humidity 10-85%
    Power Source ....   115 or 230 volts
    Heat Output ....   1500 BTU's/hr

We are heavily involved in ensuring th. the design of each model meets the specific need of our customers. Please let us know your needs.

                                      Yours faithfully
                                      EASTWAYS DEVELOPMENT (UK) LTD

                                      Amir Khan
                                      Sales Manager

For an explanation of semi-blocked letters with displayed matter, see TYPING FIRST COURSE, 5/E, page 161.

TABULATION — HORIZONTAL CENTRING

29. **Target Time: 6 minutes**

Type the following exercise on A5 landscape paper. Type the heading on the 14th single space from the top of the paper and use double spacing.

SOCIETIES AND INSTITUTIONS

Royal National Institute for the Blind   Press Association

British Gliding Association   Victorian Society

British Insurance Brokers' Association   The Samaritans

The Multiple Sclerosis Society   Royal School of Needlework

30. **Target Time: 7 minutes**

Type the following exercise on A5 landscape paper. Type the heading on the 13th single space from the top of the paper and use double spacing.

HISTORIC BUILDINGS

City of London

Bank of England   Houses of Parliament   Buckingham Palace

Dr Johnson's House   Guildhall   Lambeth Palace

Chelsea Royal Hospital   Mansion House   Kensington Palace

31. **Target Time: 6 minutes**

Type the following exercise on A5 portrait paper. Type the heading on the 20th single space from the top of the paper and use double spacing.

CONTENTS

Abbreviations   Allocating Space
Business Letters   Display
Envelopes   Footnotes
Memoranda   Paragraph Headings
Proofreading   Side Headings

Embolden the main headings and use the automatic underline feature when typing the above exercises.

For an explanation of tabulation — horizontal centring, see TYPING FIRST COURSE, 5/E, page 80.

DISPLAYED MATTER IN SEMI-BLOCKED LETTER

96. Target Time: **12 minutes**

Using A4 headed paper, type the following letter from Eastways Developments (UK) Ltd in semi-blocked style with full punctuation. Take a carbon copy, centre the subject heading and use suitable margins.

Our Ref   AK/PAC/Disk2/398   19 September 1988

Your Ref

Mrs. R. F. Delaney,
7 West Bristol Rd.,
LUDLOW,
Shropshire.
SY8 1JY

Dear Madam,

AUTUMN SALE

Thank you for your letter dated 14 September enquiring about our 'Exquisite' kitchens.

We supply everything you need in one package: base units, wall units, work tops, sink and mixer taps, oven, hob, cooker hood & fridge. The finish can be space-age laminate or warm and traditional wood, or a combination of both. The following models are being offered at less than half price:

   Star System Nine   White Worktop   £850*
   Star System Ten   Country Oak Worktop   £1,195
   Star System Eleven   White Wood/Laminate   £1,400

   * All prices include VAT

[Insert standard paragraph — SP10 — fr. p.76]

Yours faithfully,
EASTWAYS DEVELOPMENTS (U.K.) LTD.

Amir Khan
Sales Manager

Key in the above exercise (filename SALE) for 12-pitch print-out. Use bold print and automatic centring device for subject heading, provide a second left margin for the displayed portion, the indent function/indent tab setting for the indented paragraphs, and the automatic underline for the words underlined. When you have completed this exercise, turn to page 75 and follow instructions for text editing.

For an explanation of displayed matter in semi-blocked letters, see TYPING FIRST COURSE, 5/E, page 161.

TABULATION — HORIZONTAL AND VERTICAL CENTRING

32. **Target Time: 7 minutes**

Type the following exercise on A5 landscape paper. Use double spacing and leave three spaces between the columns. Centre the table vertically and horizontally.

SPELLING TEST

recommend	definitely	approximately
responsible	departments	accommodation
advertisements	guarantee	necessary
committee	receipt	companies

33. **Target Time: 8 minutes**

Type the following exercise on A5 portrait paper. Use single spacing and leave three spaces between columns. Centre the table vertically and horizontally.

C A S T

In order of appearance

Mayor	Martin Buller
First Professor	Keith Mitchelmore
Girl next door	Vanessa Young
Mother of girl next door	Susan Khan
Mayor's wife	Jo Wong
Guard	Dan Hart
Second Professor	Paul Wayne

34. **Target Time: 8 minutes**

Type the following exercise on A5 landscape paper. Use double spacing and leave three spaces between the columns. Centre the table vertically and horizontally.

TRAINING OFFICE ROTA

Monday	Pamela Neil	Morning
Tues.	Wendy McNichol	Afternoon
Wed.	Jacinta Styles	All day
Thur.	Marianne Cooper	All day
Fri.	Lubna Sherrin	Morning

Embolden the main headings and use the automatic underline feature when typing the above exercises.

For an explanation of tabulation — vertical centring, see TYPING FIRST COURSE, 5/E, page 81.

SEMI-BLOCKED LETTER WITH ATTENTION LINE, ENCLOSURE, AND SUBJECT HEADING

95.   Target Time: 15 minutes

Using A4 headed paper, type the following letter from Eastways Developments (UK) Ltd in semi-blocked style with full punctuation. Take a carbon copy and centre the subject heading. Use suitable margins.

Our Ref. AK/PAC/Disk 3/397   16 Sept. 1988

Your Ref.

FOR THE ATTENTION OF ~~MISS K. S. JUKES~~ MR. A. ADAMS

Send to: H Becket & Co Ltd — address on page 50

OFFICE FURNITURE

Thank you for your tel. enquiry of yesterday.

    Fr. the enclosed catalogue you wl. see that we are offering some very fine Secretarial L-shaped Workstations. These L-shaped layouts can be created w. the return in left- or right-hand positions, and the single-pedestal desk can be supplied w'out the return unit.

    Also, on page 4, you wl. see a range of Executive Desks wh. are in crown cut mahogany, and finished in a bright rosewood colour. The veneers hv. bn. specially selected and matched, & feature the grain pattern for which crown cut mahogany is famous.

Insert standard para — Sp9 — from p.76

This range includes a group of storage & filing cabinets wh. wl. grace any office.

                            Yours faithfully,
                            EASTWAYS DEVELOPMENTS (UK) LTD.

                            Amir Khan
                            Sales Manager

Key in the above exercise (filename FURN) for 10-pitch print-out. Use bold print for the ATTENTION line, bold print and the automatic centring device for the subject heading, and the indent function/indent tab setting for the indented paragraphs. When you have completed this exercise, turn to page 75 and follow instructions for text editing.

For an explanation of semi-blocked letters with the attention line, enclosure and subject heading, see TYPING FIRST COURSE, 5/E, page 160.

TABULATION — COLUMN HEADINGS

35. Target Time: 10 minutes

Type the following exercise in double spacing on A5 landscape paper. Leave three spaces between the columns. Centre the table vertically and horizontally. Find the monetary units for France and Mexico in Whitaker's Almanack and insert them in the tabulation when you type it.

CURRENCIES OF THE WORLD

Country	Monetary Unit	Country	Monetary Unit
Australia	Dollar	India	Rupee
Denmark	Krone	Japan	Yen
France		Mexico	

36. Target Time: 10 minutes

Type the following exercise in double spacing on A5 portrait paper. Leave three spaces between the columns. Centre the table vertically and horizontally.

POEMS AND POETS

Poet	Poem
Robert Browning	My Last Duchess
Alfred, Lord Tennyson	The Miller's Daughter
William Wordsworth	The Daffodils
William Blake	The Tyger
A E Housman	Bredon Hill

37. Target Time: 10 minutes

Type the following exercise in double spacing on A5 landscape paper. Leave three spaces between the columns. Centre the table vertically and horizontally. Change all the times to the 24-hour clock.

RADIO PROGRAMMES

Time	Programme	Station
0600	News	Radio 4
6.10 am	Farming Today	Radio 4
6.25 am	Prayer for the Day	Radio 4
6.30 am	Today	Radio 4
7.00 am	Desert Island Discs	Radio 4

Embolden the main headings and use the automatic underline feature when typing the above exercises.

For an explanation of tabulation with column headings, see TYPING FIRST COURSE, 5/E, page 82.

SEMI-BLOCKED LETTER

94. Target Time: **7 minutes**

Type the following semi-blocked letter from Eastways Developments (UK) Ltd on headed A5 portrait paper. Use open punctuation.

Our Ref AK/PAC/Disk3/396   14 Sept. 1988

W E King Esq
George King and Co Ltd
14 High Street
LEOMINSTER
Herefordshire
HR6 8LR

Dear Mr King

　　Thank you for yr letter dated 12 Sept. enquiring abt. Electronic Typewriters.

　　Our Galaxy Electronic Typewriters hv bn designed to produce work to the highest possible standard &, at the same time, they are simple to operate & very cost-effective.

　　The Galaxy has a minimum correction memory of 500 characters and this makes text modification quite simple.

[From page 76 take standard paragraph -Sp 7- & insert here.]

　　　　　　　　　Yours sincerely

　　　　　　　　　Amir Khan
　　　　　　　　　Sales Manager

Key in the above exercise (filename GALA) for 12-pitch print-out. Use bold print for the post town and the words 'Electronic Typewriters' (both cases), and the indent function/indent tab setting for the indented paragraphs. When you have completed this exercise, turn to page 75 and follow instructions for text editing.

For an explanation of semi-blocked letters, see TYPING FIRST COURSE, 5/E, page 159.

SUMS OF MONEY IN COLUMNS WITH DOUBLE UNDERSCORING OF TOTALS

38.   **Target Time: 18 minutes**

Display the following exercise on A5 landscape paper in double spacing. Leave three spaces between columns. Centre the table vertically and horizontally. Calculate and insert the missing total.

AUGUST SALES - 1988

Branch	Estimated	Actual
	£	£
Aberdeen	20,000.00	19,468.60
Birmingham	25,000.00	23,892.00
Cardiff	22,000.00	22,141.48
Glasgow	18,000.00	15,621.00
London	40,000.00	45,640.32
Manchester	22,000.00	22,821.82
Norwich	<u>13,000.00</u>	<u>15,762.00</u>
Total Sales	160.000.00	
	═══════	═══════

39.   **Target Time: 15 minutes**

Display the following exercise on A5 landscape paper in double spacing. Leave three spaces between columns. Centre the table vertically and horizontally. Calculate and insert the missing totals.

MILVERTON COLLEGE OF FURTHER EDUCATION

Budget for the year - 1988

Item	Winter Term	Spring Term	Summer Term
	£	£	£
Equipment	1,500.00	750.00	500.00
Books	650.50	325.75	200.00
Stationery	320.25	280.00	160.00
Furniture	<u>800.00</u>	<u>520.00</u>	<u>1,000.00</u>
Total	3,270.75		
	═══════	═══════	═══════

Embolden the main headings and use the automatic underline feature when typing the above exercises.

For an explanation of sums of money in columns with double underscoring of totals, see TYPING FIRST COURSE, 5/E, page 89.

INDENTED PARAGRAPHS AND SHOULDER HEADINGS

93. **Target Time: 8 minutes**

Type the following exercise on A4 paper in open punctuation. Use double spacing with double between the indented paragraphs. The words *Article(s)* and *Act* should both start with a capital *A*.

KENKOTT SCOTIA PLC

Changes in articles of Association

RIGHTS ATTACHED TO NEW SHARES

The present article 15 refers only to preference shares being issued on terms th. they may be redeemed. New article 15 now permits redemption of any shares.

ALLOTMENT OF SHARES

The issue and allotment of new shares by the Company is now subject to Section 80 and 89 of the act.

MINIMUM SUBSCRIPTION

Section 101 of the act provides th. a public company sh. not allot any share unless paid up at least as to one quarter of the nominal amount and the whole of any premium on it.

QUORUM AT GENERAL MEETINGS

New article 69 reflects the act and reduces the quorum required for general meetings from 5 members (as in the existing articles) present in person or by proxy and entitled to vote, to 2 such members.

ADJOURNED MEETINGS

There is no change in Article 70.

For an explanation of shoulder headings, see TYPING FIRST COURSE, 5/E, page 157.

PRINTED FORMS

40. Target Time: 15 minutes

There is a skeleton of the form below in the HANDBOOK AND SOLUTIONS MANUAL, 5/E, and copies may be duplicated. Insert the form into your typewriter and then type in the handwritten words.

CLAIM FORM P2430

Please read the conditions of your policy before completing the form.

Policy No HJK/424/Pers

Name of insured Mavis K LINAKER

Address 12 Heathfield Rise

CHELMSFORD Essex Postcode CM1 1FB

Telephone number (where you can be reached between 9.0 am and 5.0 pm)

0245 2662

Situation where loss, damage or injury occurred

The bracelet was lost between the office where I am employed in Chelmsford High Street & my home address.

Date of loss, damage or injury 16 Aug. 1988

Explain fully how the loss, damage or injury occurred

I was wearing my bracelet when I left home on the morning of 16 August & discovered th. it was missing when I arrived at the office 30 minutes later. I hv reported the loss to the police.

Details of article for which claim is made	Date purchased	Present replacement cost	Amount claimed
Gold bracelet	1956	£500	£500

Signature of insured ....

Date 20 August 1988

For an explanation of typing on printed forms, see TYPING FIRST COURSE, 5/E, page 90.

INDENTED PARAGRAPH HEADINGS

92.   **Target Time: 15 minutes**

Type the following exercise on A4 paper in open punctuation. Use single spacing with double between the indented paragraphs. Use upper case for the paragraph headings and do not underline. Centre the main heading and leave two clear spaces after the paragraph heading before typing the text. Use suitable margins and correct words that are circled.

```
                    HELP FOR THE SMALL INVESTOR
                                              increasingly
      GOVERNMENT SCHEME  Shareholding is an pop-
ular option, &, since the Gov. announced its pro-
posals for Personal Equity Plans (PEPs) last yr., many
people, up and down the country, hv. decided to join this
scheme.

      TAX FREE  This Gov.-encouraged plan, which began
on 1 January 1987, allows a person to invest up to £2,400
a year in industry, entirely free of tax on dividents and
capitals gains.

      A NATION OF SHAREHOLDERS  When the Gov. announced
the plan early in 1986, its long-term intention was, & is,
to encourage a nation of shareholders, allowing men &
women to hv. a personal stake in the ownership of British
firms whose products & services are household names.

      SHARE THE PROFITS  Personal Equity Plans will give us
all a chance to share in the profits of British Companies    lc
without having to pay tax.
                                                  in full
      CURRANT PLAN  The first yr. of an individual's PEP is
called the Current Plan & it runs on a calendar basis, ie,
1 January to 31 December.  You can contribute at any time
during a 'Current Plan' yr. to a max. of £2,400.

      HOLDING PLAN  At the end of the yr., all the invest-
ment, interest payments & dividends are transferred to a
Holding Plan wh. is the second year.


HAL/QB/WP 4/72
←14 September 1988
```

Key in the above exercise (filename PLAN) for 12-pitch print-out. Use bold type for paragraph headings, the automatic underline for the words underlined, and the indent function/indent tab setting for the indented paragraphs. When you have completed the exercise, turn to page 75 and follow instructions for text editing.

For an explanation of indented paragraph headings, see TYPING FIRST COURSE, 5/E, page 157.

PRINTED FORMS

41. Target Time: 12 minutes

There is a skeleton of the form below in the HANDBOOK AND SOLUTIONS MANUAL, 5/E, and copies may be duplicated. Insert the form into your typewriter and then type in the handwritten words.

ENROLMENT FORM 1988/1989

(Please use BLOCK CAPITALS)

Course Number	Course Title
MCP/24E	Microprocessor Application Course
FTA/SCT	A-level in Computer Science
Key/6EC	Keyboarding - Beginners

Surname **HOLTROPP** Title (Mr, Mrs, etc) **MR**

Forename(s) **Henri**

Street **26 The Leys**

Town **NORWICH** Postcode **NR1 3NG**

Home telephone number **Norwich 0620**

Place of work **A R Matthews & Son, Builders**

Address **Wattis Square High Street**
NORWICH NR3 8BL

Age at 31 August 1988

* 16 ☐   17 ☐   18 ☐   19 ☑   20-59 ☐   60-69 ☐   70+ ☐

I enclose a cheque for £ **45.00**

Signed _____ Date **14 September 1988**

* Please tick as appropriate

For an explanation of typing on printed forms, see TYPING FIRST COURSE, 5/E, page 90.

HEADINGS CENTRED IN THE TYPING LINE

91. Target Time: 12 minutes

Type the following exercise on A4 paper in double spacing. Use indented paragraphs and centre the main heading and subheadings in the typing line. Margins: 12 pitch 20-85, 10 pitch 11-76.

H O L I D A Y S   I N   I R E L A N D

<u>Dublin Weekends</u>

Get away fr. it all w. a 2-night weekend break to Dublin. W. so much to see and do, we are sure you wl. find our hotels are in ideal locations; they are in the heart of Dublin City beside shops, museums & *theatres,* places of *historic* interest.

Your holiday includes:

1   By sea:

    (a)   return ferry with own car

    (b)   accommodation based on twin occupancy for a minimum of 2 nights [leave one clear space]

    (c)   room with private bath/shower & colour TV

    (d)   *full Irish breakfast ea. day*

2   By air:

    (a)   return air travel to Dublin

    (b)   as for 1 (b), (c), & (d) above.

<u>A Different Kind of Holiday</u>

For those of you who like *variety*, may we *say* th. the best way to discover Ireland is for you to decide fr. day to day where you wish to stay - see the hotels listed on page 5. All you have to do is choose where you wish to stop on yr first night. *After th. you are free to decide ea. day at wh. hotel you wish to stay.*

Key in the above exercise (filename HOLS) for 12-pitch print-out. Use the automatic centring function for the centred heading. Utilize the indent function/second margins/indent tab settings for the indented paragraphs and numbered items, and the automatic underline for the words underlined. Embolden the main heading. When you have completed the exercise, turn to page 75 and follow instructions for text editing.

For an explanation of centred headings, see TYPING FIRST COURSE, 5/E, page 156.

FORM LETTERS

42.   Target Time: **10 minutes**

Using a printed form letter from the HANDBOOK AND SOLUTIONS MANUAL, 5/E, type in the following handwritten details.

W M ELECTRONICS

Deerpark   BELFAST   BT1 1AA
Telephone 0232 644223   Telex 99783

Your Ref   H/43126
Our Ref   PMA/JF

18 July 1988

Mrs Pat O'Donavon
26 Kiln Rd
Lurgan
Craigavon
Co Armagh

Dear ~~Sir~~/Madam

May we remind you that the annual servicing of your Electronic washing machine, and central heating unit is now due, and we would like our engineer to call on Tuesday, 26 July 1988 at 2.00 pm to attend to this.

Should this date not be suitable, an alternative would be Tuesday, 2 August 1988 at 10.00 am. The charge for servicing will be £50.00

Yours faithfully
W M ELECTRONICS

43.   Target Time: **10 minutes**

Using another copy of the printed form letter, insert the following details.

Your Ref T/4621   Our Ref PMA/JF   Date 21 July 1988
Addressee Mr L Conway, 81 Downpatrick Rd, Killyleach, Co Down
To be serviced Electronic dishwasher, central heating unit + fridge/freezer
To call on Mon 8 Aug '88; 11am   Alternative date Wed 24 Aug; 2.30 pm
Charge for servicing £75.00

For an explanation of form letters, see TYPING FIRST COURSE, 5/E, page 92.

HORIZONTAL CENTRING — ALL LINES CENTRED

89. Target Time: **6 minutes**

Type the following notice on A5 landscape paper. Set a tab stop at the horizontal centre point of the page and centre each line horizontally and the whole notice vertically.

<pre>
                      IN-CAR ENTERTAINMENT

                    Electronic Combination Unit

                       LW/MW/FM Stereo Radio
                               with
                     FIVE-BAND GRAPHIC EQUALIZER
                               and
                           AUTO REVERSE

                 Twenty watts maximum output power
</pre>

90. Target Time: **10 minutes**

Type the following notice on A5 portrait paper. Centre horizontally and the whole notice vertically.

<pre>
              L E E   G A R D E N S   H O T E L
              Causeway Bay   HONG KONG ISLAND

                  900 Bedrooms and 9 lifts   UC

                  The Exotic Charm of the East
                              and
                        Western Comfort

                     R E S T A U R A N T S

                    Okahan - Japanese Style
                  Pavilion - Continental Cuisine
                  Rainbow Room - Chinese Dishes
                    GoGu Jang - Korean Food

                            CAFÉ
</pre>

Key in exercise 90 (filename FOOD) for 10-pitch print-out. Use bold type for the heading: LEE GARDENS HOTEL, the automatic centring device and the automatic underline key for the words underlined. When you have completed this exercise, turn to page 74 and follow instructions for text editing.

For an explanation of horizontal centring with all lines centred, see TYPING FIRST COURSE, 5/E, page 154.

INVOICES — VALUED ADDED TAX (VAT)

44. Target Time: **15 minutes**

Please complete an invoice from the following particulars. A skeleton invoice form is given in the HANDBOOK AND SOLUTIONS MANUAL, 5/E.

Seller Casa de Europa PLC

Buyer G V Latham & Co Ltd
8 Monks Road
North Hykeham
LINCOLN   LN6 9QX

Invoice No 4689
dated 26 October 1988

Tax point 26.10.88
Type of supply Sale

Your Order No Disk 38/389/88   **Account No** L/372   **Advice Note No** 6672

4	Executive Document Cases	£75.00	£300.00
2	Executive Briefcases	£100.00	£200.00
5	Boxes Lift off Tapes	£4.00	£20.00

VAT SUMMARY

Code	%	Goods	Tax
1	15	£520.00	£78.00

Total Goods please calculate and insert
Discount £0.00
Total VAT £78.00
TOTAL please calculate and insert

45. Target Time: **15 minutes**

Please complete an invoice from the following particulars. A skeleton invoice is given in the HANDBOOK AND SOLUTIONS MANUAL, 5/E.

Seller Casa de Europa PLC

Invoice No. 4690
dated 26 Oct. 88

Buyer W M Leonard & Sons
1 Green Road
STOKE-ON-TRENT
SL6 8LT

Tax point 26.10.88

Type of supply Sale

Your Order No. 279/88

Account No. M 380

Advice Note No. 6673

10	Reams A4 White 80 gsm	£3.00	£30.00
10	Reams A4 White 45 gsm	£2.50	£25.00
10	Reams A5 White 70 gsm	£2.00	£20.00

VAT SUMMARY

Code	%	Goods	Tax
1	15	£75.00	£11.25

Total goods Please total & insert
Discount £0.00
Total VAT £11.25
TOTAL Please calculate & insert

For an explanation of invoices, see TYPING FIRST COURSE, 5/E, page 96.

PARAGRAPHING — BLOCKED, INDENTED AND HANGING

86. Target Time: 6 minutes

Type the following exercise on A5 landscape paper with margins of 12 pitch 22-82, 10 pitch 12-72. Use blocked paragraphs.

CELLULAR PHONES

Cellular telephones should not be confused with cordless telephones. Cellular phones are used mainly in motor cars while the cordless phone can be utilized only within a short radius.

Car telephones must not be used on motorways because it is illegal to make or receive telephone calls in a moving vehicle, & it is illegal for a driver to stop on the motorway (hard shoulder) to make or take a telephone call, except in an emergency. The instant fine is at present £24, & if the driver decided to go to court, it may cost her/him £400.

87. Target Time: 7 minutes

Type the following exercise on A5 portrait paper with margins of 12 pitch 13-63, 10 pitch 6-56. Use indented paragraphs and centre the main and subheading.

C R E D I T   C A R D S

The Easiest Way to Pay

    Your credit card is a way of paying that can do away with conventional cheque and cash transactions. It is probably the most flexible way of handling your finances.

    There are at least a dozen very good reasons for having a credit card. You can use it for personal or business expenditure, and for paying regular bills. You can buy now and pay later!

    A word of warning: keep a careful check on yr. payments so that you do not overspend.

88. Target Time: 5 minutes

Type the following exercise on A5 portrait paper with margins of 12 pitch 15-65, 10 pitch 6-56. Use hanging paragraphs and block the main heading.

ADVANTAGES OF THE CREDIT CARD SYSTEM

    Your card will be accepted in more than 5 million outlets throughout the world.

    It costs nothing to obtain one and, with careful planning, will cost nothing to run.

    It is a very convenient substitute for conventional cheque & cash transactions.

For an explanation of blocked, indented and hanging paragraphs, see TYPING FIRST COURSE, 5/E, page 152.

CREDIT NOTES

46. Target Time: 15 minutes

Please complete a credit note from the following particulars. A skeleton form is given in the HANDBOOK AND SOLUTIONS MANUAL, 5/E. Take a carbon copy.

From Casa de Europa PLC   **To** G V Latham & Co Ltd
(take address from previous page)

Credit Note No 2754   **Date** 17 November 1988
Original tax invoice No 4689   **Date of invoice** 26.10.88

Reason for credit Damaged in transit   **Quantity** 1
Description Executive Document Case   **Total** £75.00

Total Credit £75.00   **Plus VAT** £11.25   **TOTAL** please calculate and insert

VAT SUMMARY

Code	%	Goods	Tax
1	15	£75.00	£11.25

47. Target Time: 15 minutes

Please complete a credit note from the following particulars. A skeleton form is given in the HANDBOOK AND SOLUTIONS MANUAL, 5/E.

From Casa de Europa PLC   To W M Leonard & Sons
(Take address for previous page.)

Credit Note No. 2755
Original Tax Invoice No. 4690   Date 18 Nov. 88
Date of Invoice 26.10.88

Reason for credit Short delivery   Quantity 2 Reams
Description A4 White 45 gsm   Total £5.00

Total Credit   Please calculate & enter
Plus VAT   Please enter
TOTAL   Please enter

VAT SUMMARY

Code	%	Goods	Tax
1	15	£5.00	£0.75

For an explanation of credit notes, see TYPING FIRST COURSE, 5/E, page 97.

FULLY-BLOCKED LETTER WITH FULL PUNCTUATION AND DISPLAY

85. Target Time: 12 minutes

Type the following letter in fully-blocked style with full punctuation on suitable letterhead paper (Kenkott Scotia PLC). Take a carbon copy and type a suitable envelope.

Please insert complimentary close, & correct the words that are circled.

Our Ref. BL/MAD

12 Dec. 1988

FOR THE ATTENTION OF MS. R. L. BARTON

Send to J. D. Mead PLC - address on p. 50

Dear Sirs,

Thank you for yr. letter dated 9 Dec. enquiring abt. acoustic screens for yr. open-plan office.

We hv. pleasure in enclosing a copy of our catalogue & wd. draw yr. attention to the offer on page 14. These linked screens are upholstered in Wool/Tweed Heather or Corn colour with brown linking & (ajustable) brown legs.

The following sizes (is) on special offer:

AS/21	1000 x 1500 mm	Heather	£144.55
AS/30	1250 x 1500 mm	Heather	£149.30
AS/32	1250 x 1835 mm	Corn	£150.60
AS/39	1650 x 1835 mm	Corn	£163.42

Insert here para. fr. p. 76 starting 'Our experts ...'

BRIAN LUCKNOWE
SALES MANAGER

Key in the above exercise (filename FURN) for 10-pitch print-out. Use bold type for the ATTENTION LINE. When you have completed this exercise, turn to page 74 and follow instructions for text editing.

For an explanation of a fully-blocked letter with full punctuation and display, see TYPING FIRST COURSE, 5/E, page 145.

ENUMERATED ITEMS

48.　　　　　　　　　　　　　　　　　　　　　　　　　　　Target Time: 12 minutes

Type the following on A4 paper in single spacing with double between the numbered items.
Margins: 12 pitch 22-82, 10 pitch 12-72.

M I N U T E S

Minutes are an accurate record of the proceedings of a meeting and are kept so that a brief record is preserved. It is the secretary's duty to attend the meeting and take the minutes which should be typed in the following order:

1　Place, date and time of the meeting.

2　Name and/or numbers of those present.

3　Apologies for absence.

4　Minutes of the last meeting.

5　Matters arising from the minutes.

6　Any correspondence.

7　The main business - which must include a verbatim record of any resolutions passed.

8　Any other business.

9　Date of next meeting.

49.　　　　　　　　　　　　　　　　　　　　　　　　　　　Target Time: 10 minutes

Type the following on A4 paper in single spacing with double between the numbered items.
Margins: 12 pitch 22-82, 10 pitch 12-72.

The Annual General Meeting of Pilkington Engineering plc, Sports & Social Club, w/ be held in the Conference Hall on Tues., 12 Sept. 1988 at 1830 hrs.

A G E N D A

1　Apologies for absence
2　The minutes of the A—G—M— held on 2 Sept. '87
3　Matters arising out of the minutes
4　Correspondence
5　Annual Reports
6　Election of Officers
7　Film of Wimbledon Finals '88
8　Date of next A—G—M—

Embolden words in spaced capitals and use the automatic underline feature when typing the above exercises.

For an explanation of enumerated items, see TYPING FIRST COURSE, 5/E, page 99.

FULL PUNCTUATION — ABBREVIATIONS AND FORMS OF ADDRESS

82. Target Time: 6 minutes

Type the following sentences on A5 landscape paper in single spacing with full punctuation. Margins: 12 pitch 20-80, 10 pitch 12-72.

```
The desk for Mrs. R. E. Nash's office measures 3 ft.
11 in. wide x 2 ft. 5½ in. down (1193.80 x 749.00 mm).

Make certain the VDU Work Table is the correct size:
2 ft. 7½ in. wide x 2 ft. 5½ in. x 2 ft. 4½ in. high,
i.e., 800.00 x 745.50 x 724.00 mm.

H. C. L. Carson, Esq., said that most of our products
are marked with imperial and metric weights, e.g.,
coffee 200 gm or 7.05 oz.; salt 3.31 lb. or 1.50 kg.
Other equivalents: 1 yd. cloth = 0.91 m; 1 ft. = 0.30 m.
```

83. Target Time: 6 minutes

Type the following sentences on A5 portrait paper in single spacing with full punctuation. Margins: 12 pitch 13-63, 10 pitch 6-56.

```
Mr. and Mrs. B. M. Murray live at 2 St. Mary's Road,
Coventry, W. Midlands, CV4 9FR.

Call on Ms. T. U. Carter, M.D., B.Ch., at 10 a.m. or about
2.15 p.m.  She leaves the clinic at 4.10 p.m.

The Rt. Hon. James St. George-Stephens, M.P., will call on
Admiral Sir Robert Broadhurst, G.B.E., D.S.O., at 1500 hrs.

Messrs. A. J. Cleary & Co. changed its name to A. J. Cleary
& Co. Ltd. in 1976; now the organization is known as A. J.
Cleary P.L.C.
```

84. Target Time: 10 minutes

Type C6 envelopes to the following. Use blocked style and full punctuation. Mark the envelope to H. Becket & Co. Ltd. 'FOR THE ATTENTION OF MR. A. ADAMS', and the envelope to D. J. Barry, Junior, '<u>PERSONAL</u>'. Do not copy the single quotation marks.

```
H. Becket & Co. Ltd., 21 Market Street, WHITEHAVEN, Cumbria.  CA28 7JD
Miss K. McD. Burns, 5 High Street, INVERGORDON, Ross-shire.  IV18 0DE
D. J. Barry, Esq., Junior, 9 Swansea Road, LLANELLI, Dyfed.  SA15 4HR
Mrs. R. Q. Lucas, M.B.E., 3 Australia Road, POOLE, Dorset.  BH15 1AA
J. D. Mead P.L.C., Cumberland Way, MORDEN, Surrey.  SY10 9NW
Dr. J. K. O'Connell, Castle View, Church Hill, SLIGO, Irish Republic.
Rev. N. Jamieson, D.D., The Rectory, Oxford Street, SUNDERLAND.  SR1  1AA
Mr. L. M. McCabe, 14 Market Square, ARMAGH.  BT61 7AA
Señor José Santamaria, Calle Islas Baleares 35, Alicante, SPAIN.
```

For an explanation of full punctuation — abbreviations and forms of address, see TYPING FIRST COURSE, 5/E, pages 142-144.

INSET MATTER

50. Target Time: 10 minutes

Type the following on A5 landscape paper in single spacing with double between the lettered items. Margins: 12 pitch 22-82, 10 pitch 12-72.

THE WORK OF THE UNITED NATIONS

The United Nations came into being towards the end of the second world war. It has more than 100 member nations with its headquarters in New York. Its aims are to maintain international peace, and to encourage improved economic and social conditions throughout the world.

The United Nations works through a number of subsidiary organizations and specialist agencies. Among these are:

    A   United Nations Educational, Scientific and Cultural Organization - UNESCO

    B   United Nations Children's Fund - UNICEF

    C   World Health Organization - WHO

    D   International Monetary Fund - IMF

51. Target Time: 12 minutes

Type the following on A4 paper in single spacing with double between the lettered items. Margins: 12 pitch 22-82, 10 pitch 12-72.

WORD PROCESSORS

Word processing systems vary greatly in their mode of operation, but all have the QWERTY keyboard and groups of extra keys to perform various functions, such as —

(Inset 12 spaces)

    a) Centre
    b) bold
    c) insert
    d) delete
    e) edit
    f) select

Other w— pr— use a combination of function/letter or number keys to perform the above + other functions. It is, therefore, necessary for even the experienced word processor operator to spend some time getting to know his or her individual machine.

Embolden the main heading; set a temporary, second left margin or use indent function/indent tab setting for inset portion; and use the word wraparound function when typing the above exercises.

For an explanation of inset matter, see TYPING FIRST COURSE, 5/E, page 100.

ALLOCATING SPACE

81. Target Time: 12 minutes

Type the following letter from Eastways Developments (UK) Ltd on plain A4 paper with margins of 12 pitch 22-82, 10 pitch 12-72. It will be sent to about 40 selected customers next week. As all the information is not available, leave spaces where indicated, so that the details may be added before the final typing.

(Leave 8 clear spaces at the top)

Our Ref   RESEARCH/Disk23A/10/178

23 October 1988

(Leave space for name & address)

Dear

DIGITAL TELEPHONE SYSTEM

Our new PACIFIC keypad clearly describes what every button is there for. Within a couple of days of the system being installed, everyone will be at ease with all the system's capabilities. Our prices are as follows:

(Leave a minimum of 2" (51 mm)) You can start with just 2 lines and 4 extensions, and, with almost no disturbance, expand it up to 12 lines and at least 32 extensions.

By furnishing you with a wide variety of ways to make contact, and by providing a keypad that tells you precisely what is happening at that particular moment on any extension, we give you a system that is adaptable and simple to understand.

Over the years we have accumulated a vast amount of valuable experience / in the mfr of digital telephone systems. Also, we know th first-class service is valued more than / reductions. / price

Modern electronics has brought advantages to business, ie, as equipment has become smaller, the number of features it offers has grown. However, is often more true than at the office telephone.

(Leave a minimum of 1½" (38 mm))

(Typist - omit complimentary close)

Set a second margin/indent function/tab facility for the paragraph starting 'You can...', and use bold type for the subject heading. Justify the right margin. When you have completed this exercise, turn to page 74 and follow instructions for text editing.

For an explanation of allocating space, see TYPING FIRST COURSE, 5/E, page 139.

ENVELOPE ADDRESSING

52. **Target Time: 7 minutes**

Type the following addresses on DL envelopes. Mark the first envelope CONFIDENTIAL and the second FOR THE ATTENTION OF MR JOSEPH ZAMAN.

Mrs Patricia R Hamlett   4 Royal Crescent   NORWICH   Norfolk   NR1 4AA
Zaman Bros   Shore Road   Ventnor   ISLE OF WIGHT   PO38 2HA
Ms B Desai   20 Overcliff Drive   Southbourne   BOURNEMOUTH   Dorset   BH6 3N6
Rev Paul Flaherty   Main Street   IRVINESTOWN   Co Fermanagh   BT74 9XX
A M Magnus Esq   Angus Road   Wormit   NEWPORT ON TAY   Fife   DD6 8RD
Sir Frank Coggins   Honeysuckle Cottage   Bellingham   HEXHAM   Northd   NE48 2JZ
Mr and Mrs J Bignell   30 North Street   BUILTH WELLS   Powys   LD2 3TF
Mr M P Hanrahan   57 Fidlas Road   Llanishan   CARDIFF   CF4 5LZ

Special note

From this point on in the textbook a number of exercises will be incomplete, and it will be necessary for you to find and extract the information from page 76, and insert it in the appropriate place in the exercise.

53. **Target Time: 12 minutes**

Type the following letter from Eastways Developments (UK) Ltd on A5 letterhead paper. Margins: 12 pitch 13-63, 10 pitch 5-56. Type a DL envelope and mark the letter and envelope URGENT. The letter is to be addressed to Mr Hanrahan. His address is given in the previous exercise.

Our ref FRS/PL

11 July 1988

Dr Householder

We are specialists in exterior wall treatments, & during the next few weeks we wl. be making visits to yr. area, viewing a no. of properties to assist in the necy. advertising & promotion of our services.

(Type Standard Paragraph —Sp 11— from p 76, at this point.)

We look forward to hearing fr. you.

Yrs. ffy.
EASTWAYS DEVELOPMENTS (UK) LTD

F R SALIM
Publicity Dept.

Embolden the word URGENT and use the word wraparound function.

Special note

You may wish to key in and store the sentences from page 76. You can then retrieve them as and when required.

For an explanation about typing of envelopes, see TYPING FIRST COURSE, 5/E, page 103.

ALLOCATING SPACE

80. Target Time: **12 minutes**

Type the following on A4 paper in single spacing with margins of 12 pitch 41-82, 10 pitch 31-72. Set tab stop for start of side headings.

SENIOR CITIZEN RAILCARD

There are 2 kinds of Senior Citizen Railcard - one costs £12 and the other £7. The £12 card offers the following facilities:

ONE-THIRD OFF   Available for most second-class journeys
SAVER TICKETS   over abt. 50 miles. Travel outward on
                    the day shown on the ticket & return
                    within one month.

(Leave 4 clear lines here)

HALF-PRICE CHEAP   Available for second-class journeys up
DAY RETURNS   to abt. 50 miles. Although mainly for
                    off-peak travel, the cheap day return
                    can be used any time of day in some
                    areas.

(Leave 2 clear lines here)

Word HALF-PRICE   Available for second-class journeys &
STANDARD DAY   for first class where available. Covers
RETURN   journeys up to abt. 30 miles.

(Leave 2 clear lines here)

ONE-THIRD OFF   Valid for first-class travel where avail-
STANDARD SINGLES   able.

(Leave 2 clear)

Word ONE-THIRD OFF   For first-class travel where available
STANDARD RETURNS   & for all second-class travel.

(Leave 2 clear)

OTHER BENEFITS   Reductions on certain Golden Rail Holidays.

(Leave 3 clear)

Both the £12 and £7 Railcard give these extra benefits:

(a) You can take up to 4 children at a set price per
     head extra.

(b) Some cheap underground tickets in London.

Key in the above exercise (filename TELS) for 12-pitch print-out. Set a second margin/indent function/tab facility for the start of the text and embolden the side headings. When you have completed this exercise, turn to page 74 and follow instructions for text editing.

For an explanation of allocating space, see TYPING FIRST COURSE, 5/E, page 139.

CARBON COPIES

54.   **Target Time: 15 minutes**

Type the following letter from Eastways Developments (UK) Ltd on A4 letterhead paper. Margins: 12 pitch 22-82, 10 pitch 12-72. Take a carbon copy and type a DL envelope. The letter is to be addressed to Mr and Mrs J Bignell. Their address is given in exercise 52 of this textbook.

Our ref PG/Quo2/FA

Today's date

Dr Mr & Mrs B——

PLAN & QUOTATION

Please find enclosed the revised Plan & Quotation incorporating the amendments wh we discussed.

(Inset 5 spaces)

1. Item no 11 is changed from a 400 mm wide base cupboard to a 300 mm wide base cupboard.

2. Item 24 is a 300 mm wide wall cupboard. This was unfortunately omitted from Quote B.

3. The extractor wl be vented thro' the right-hand wall.

4. I have now listed as white, all the accessories.

(Take standard paragraph —Sp1— from page 76, and insert here.)

In any case, I look forward to hearing from you soon.

(Insert a suitable complimentary close)

PAULINE GRICE

Set a temporary, second left margin or use the tabulation facility for the inset portion and embolden the subject heading.

For an explanation of typing carbon copies, see TYPING FIRST COURSE, 5/E, page 104.

SIDE HEADINGS

79.   **Target Time: 12 minutes**
Type the following on A4 paper. Follow handwritten instructions very carefully.

OFFICE FURNITURE   *margins: 12 pitch 22-82*
                                                         10 "   12-72

A Complete New Range of Chairs

The chair is perhaps the most important /single\ item of furniture in the office and worth a great deal of thought before purchase. A correctly designed chair provides support & freedom from stress during a /long\ working day.   *This paragraph in single spacing*

POSTURE CHAIR   Gas spring or mechanical seat depth & height adjustment.

DESKCHAIR 'B'   These chairs hv. only one le/a/ver to adjust both seat & back angles. Adjustable seat height w. gas spring.

DESKCHAIR 'A'   A comfortable chair ~~with~~ w. adjustable forward tilt. Seat height adjustable w. gas spring.

EXECUTIVE 'A'   High-backed chair w. adjustable tilt.

EXECUTIVE 'B'   Two different back heights. Adjustable lumber support and variable lockable tilting.

In double spacing. Set tab stop and reset margin

SOLID   *Sturdily built range of stacking chairs in oak or beech. Upholstered or wooden backs, w. or w'out armrests. Suitable for many purposes.*

Key in the above document (filename DESKS) for 12-pitch print-out. Use the automatic underline feature for the subheading, bold print for the side headings, and a second margin indent function/tab facility for the beginning of the text. When you have completed this exercise, turn to page 74 and follow instructions for text editing.

For an explanation of side headings, see TYPING FIRST COURSE, 5/E, page 138.

COLUMN DISPLAY IN FULLY-BLOCKED LETTERS

55. Target Time: 15 minutes

Type the following letter from Eastways Developments (UK) Ltd on A4 letterhead paper. Margins: 12 pitch 22-82, 10 pitch 12-72. Take a carbon copy and type a DL envelope.

8 Sept 88

Mr D Davies
58 Jacoby Place
BRIDGEND
Mid Glamorgan
CF31 1AA

My dr David

SPONSORED RUN & BARBEQUE

I am sorry you were not able to attend the Annual General Mtg of our Sports & Social Club because of ill health. As I know you were very involved in the arrangements for the sponsored run & barbeque in July, I thought you wld be interested in the way the money raised was distributed.

1 Donation to Spastics Society   £
2 Donation to Day Centre for the Elderly   £
3 Donation to St Ives's Children's Home   £

(Typist - Please take amounts from table on p 76)

All the hard work was very well worthwhile. Many thanks, & my best wishes for yr speedy recovery.

Sincerely

Use the word wraparound function and embolden the subject heading when typing the above exercise.

For an explanation of column display in fully-blocked letters, see TYPING FIRST COURSE, 5/E, page 107.

BLOCKED TABULATION — HORIZONTAL AND VERTICAL RULING

78. **Target Time: 20 minutes**

Type the following exercise in double spacing on A4 paper. Use blocked style and centre the exercise horizontally and vertically. Insert leader dots in the second column.

AIR TRAVEL LTD

<u>Departures from London Airport</u>

DATE	TO	DURATION	TARIFF
17 September	Hong Kong	23 days	£3,960
4 October	Peking ————	21 days	£2,750
20 Oct	Auckland	36 days	£4,300
1 Nov	Istanbul	32 days	£3,790
22 Nov	Santiago	31 days	£3,700
→2 Jan	St Lucia (Cap Estate)	28 days	£3,100
20 Jan.	Antigua (St John's)	14 days	£2,141
21 Feb	Jamaica (Kingston) ..	21 days	£1,980
6 Feb	Bahamas (Cruise)	21 days	£2,100
⌈3 Dec	Miami	17 days	£3,400
⌊17 Dec	Barbados (Bridgetown)	21 days	£3,222
3 March	Caribbean ——— .	28 days	£3,400
22 "	Orlando ———	21 days	£2,750

[ANTIGUA]

Key in the above exercise (filename TRAV) for 12-pitch print-out. Embolden the main heading and use the automatic underline feature for the subheading. Use the save function for the first horizontal ruled line and copy it where necessary. Also, use the vertical-line key. When you have completed this exercise, turn to page 74 and follow instructions for text editing.

For an explanation of blocked tabulation with horizontal and vertical ruling, see TYPING FIRST COURSE, 5/E, page 136.

COLUMN DISPLAY IN FULLY-BLOCKED LETTERS

56. Target Time: 15 minutes

Type the following letter from Eastways Developments (UK) Ltd on A4 letterhead paper. Margins: 12 pitch 22–82, 10 pitch 12–72. Take a carbon copy and type a C6 envelope. Mark the letter and envelope URGENT.

Our ref BW/AR

Tomorrow's date

Ms A P Hadley
62 Rue Cohu
St Helier
Jersey
Channel Islands

Dr Ms H———

PRICE LIST

I give below the items wh were omitted from the price list sent to you last week.

D191	600 Base cupboard w drawer	£90.79
D151	Tray space w telescopic towel rail	£32.00
DT600	Worktop w wood edge	£26.76

I am enclosing our latest catalogue, & apologize most sincerely for the inconvenience caused.

(Type standard paragraph – Sp3 – from page 76, at this point.)

(Insert a suitable complimentary close)

B Weiss
Sales Manager

Use the word wraparound function and embolden the subject heading when typing the above exercise.

For an explanation of fully-blocked letters with column display, see TYPING FIRST COURSE, 5/E, page 107.

BLOCKED TABULATION — HORIZONTAL AND VERTICAL RULING

76. **Target Time: 15 minutes**

Type the following exercise in double spacing on A5 portrait paper. Use blocked style and centre vertically on the paper. Leave three spaces between columns, and rule.

```
CONNECTING TRAINS FOR

Holyhead to Dublin*
```

Depart	Morning	Night
London (Euston)	1000	2200
Birmingham		
Leeds		
Manchester		
Preston		

Typist - please take times fr. table on page 76

```
* Subject to change without notice
```

77. **Target Time: 15 minutes**

Type the following table in double spacing on A5 landscape paper. Use blocked style and centre vertically on the paper. Leave three spaces between columns, and rule.

```
LEE, CLARK, AND CRADDOCK

Amazing Offers!
```

Latest Model	Feature	Sale Price
Twin-deck Hi-Fi	Graphic Equalizer	£259.99
Compact Disc Midi	Linear Track	
Computer	128K	
Word Processor	256K	
Portable TV	Remote Control	

Please take prices for table on page 76

For an explanation of blocked tabulation with horizontal and vertical ruling, see TYPING FIRST COURSE, 5/E, page 136.

SUPERSCRIPTS, SUBSCRIPTS AND ACCENTS

57. Target Time: **15 minutes**

Type the following exercise on A5 portrait paper in double spacing. Centre the exercise horizontally and vertically.

THE FORMULAE FOR SOME COMPOUNDS

Formulae	Compound
H_2O	Water
H_2SO_4	Sulphuric acid
CO_2	Carbon dioxide
SO_2	Sulphur dioxide
Na_2CO_3	Sodium carbonate
$CuSO_4$	Copper sulphate

58. Target Time: **15 minutes**

Type the following exercise on A5 landscape paper in double spacing. Margins: 12 pitch 22-82, 10 pitch 12-72.

Find the remainder (if any) which results from dividing

(1) $x^3 + 2x^2 - x + 6$ by $x - 3$

(2) $x^3 + 9x^2 + 26x + 24$ by $x + 4$

(3) $x^5 - x^4 + x^3 + 2x + 5$ by $x + 1$

(4) $x^3 = 8x^2 - 31x - 20$ by $- 11$

59. Target Time: **7 minutes**

Type the following on A5 landscape paper in double spacing. Centre the exercise horizontally and vertically. Insert the accents in ink.

FRENCH AND SPANISH

French	English
Peut-être avait-il raison.	Perhaps he was right.
Le garçon était très vieux.	The waiter was very old.

Spanish	English
Mañana por la tarde.	Tomorrow afternoon.
La señora se había levantado.	The lady had got up.

If your machine has the special symbols for accents, you may wish to use them.

For an explanation of typing superscripts, subscripts and accents, see TYPING FIRST COURSE, 5/E, page 115.

BLOCKED TABULATION — HORIZONTAL RULING

74. Target Time: 15 minutes

Type the following exercise in double spacing on A5 portrait paper. Use blocked style and centre the exercise vertically and horizontally on the paper.

POSTAL ABBREVIATIONS FOR COUNTIES

Town	County	Abbreviation
Newbury	Berkshire	
Huntingdon	Cambridgeshire	
Southsea	Hampshire	
Baldock	Hertfordshire	
Lutterworth	Leicestershire	
Ashington	Northumberland	
Swindon	Wiltshire	
Bromsgrove	Worcestershire	

Typist — please insert abbreviations

75. Target Time: 12 minutes

Type the following exercise in double spacing on A5 landscape paper in blocked style. Centre vertically and horizontally on the paper, and rule.

McGRAW-HILL BOOK COMPANY (UK) LIMITED

Business Education Books

Text	Author	Approximate Price
Computer Literacy Skills	Bishop	
Word Processing Dictionary	Dando	£3.25
The Conference	Gaukroger	
The Practical Secretary	Holmes	TBA
The Receptionist Today	Trevethin	TBA

Please take prices fr. page 76

For an explanation of tabulation with horizontal ruling, see TYPING FIRST COURSE, 5/E, page 135.

BRACE

60. Target Time: 20 minutes

Type the following exercise on A5 portrait paper in single spacing with double between each grouping. Centre the exercise horizontally and vertically.

TELEVISION PROGRAMMES

```
3.50 pm    News and Weather)
4.00 pm    My Music        )    BBC 2
4.30 pm    Tomorrow's World)
```

7.00 pm Holidays '88)
7.30 pm Eastenders   ) BBC 1
8.00 pm Film '88   )

8.00 pm Brookside   )
8.30 pm Moneyspinner   ) Channel 4
9.00 pm Channel 4 News)

61. Target Time: 7 minutes

Type the following exercise on A5 landscape paper. Use single spacing for the bracketed items with double spacing between the groups. Centre the exercise horizontally and vertically.

WEATHER

February 1988

```
Austria     )    Heavy snow showers.  Very cold.
Norway      )    Outlook: Further snow.
Sweden      )
Switzerland)
```

Holland) Sunny Spells. Cold.   l.c.
Germany) Outlook: Some snow showers
France   )

For an explanation of how to type brace, see TYPING FIRST COURSE, 5/E, page 116.

BLOCKED TABULATION — LEADER DOTS

72. **Target Time: 12 minutes**

Type the following exercise in double spacing on A5 portrait paper. Centre vertically and horizontally in blocked style and insert leader dots in columns one and two.

CASE STUDY ASSIGNMENTS IN

Secretarial Procedures

by Joanna Gaukroger

PUBLISHED BY McGRAW-HILL BOOK COMPANY (UK) LTD

EXTRACT FROM CONTENTS

Case Study No	Subject	Page No
1	Outgoing Mail	2
2	Filing and Record Keeping	5
3	Reprographics	8
5	The Telephone System	15
8	Job Applications	27
6	Health and Safety	20
21	Personnel Department	92

Insert:
11 Word Processing 42
15 Organising a Meeting 66

73. **Target Time: 10 minutes**

Type the following exercise on A5 landscape paper in blocked style. Centre horizontally and vertically. Insert leader dots.

P R I C E - L I S T

GENERAL OFFICE PRODUCTS

Stock Code	Item Description	Price
2174	Record Trays (Visible Edge)	£75.50
2875	A4 Binders	
2896	Drawer Tidy	
2900	Office Holder	
3021	Ring Binders (4 colours) ..	
3024	Box Files	£2.80

Please take prices fr. table on page 76

For an explanation of blocked tabulation with leader dots, see TYPING FIRST COURSE, 5/E, page 134.

PROOFREADERS' MARKS

62. Target Time: 20 minutes

Type a copy of the following exercise on A4 paper in double spacing. Margins: 12 pitch 22-82, 10 pitch 12-72.

THE WEST INDIES

Jamaica

It is a beautiful island with an area of 4,480 sq miles, about two-thirds the size of Wales. The population is over 1,500,000. The Blue Mountain range in eastern Jamaica has one peak which is 7,400 feet high. Columbus discovered Jamaica in 1494.

[Trs]

The north coast of Jamaica is famous for its beaches, and one of its main sources of income is from tourism. Sugar is its most important crop from which it makes the famous Jamaican Rum. [Run on]

Breadfruit is an important food. Breadfruit trees grow wild, and after the fruit is picked, it is baked and then sliced, rather like a loaf of bread.

Kingston is Jamaica's capital with a population of over 400,000. It is an important port, and the University College of the West Indies was opened here in 1948.

Key in exercise 62 (filename WINDS) for 10-pitch print-out. Embolden the main heading. When you have completed this exercise, turn to page 74 and follow instructions for text editing.

For an explanation of proofreaders' marks, see TYPING FIRST COURSE, 5/E, page 118.

BLOCKED TABULATION WITH SINGLE-LINE COLUMN HEADINGS AND FOOTNOTES

71. **Target Time: 20 minutes**

Type the following exercise on A4 paper. Centre vertically and horizontally in blocked style. Type in single spacing with double between each item.

P E R F E C T   G I F T S

HOME SHOPPING LIMITED

Gift Number	Description	Price*
		£
VT 116	Video Tape Library and Case	23.00
JT 128	(Porcelain) Japanese Tea Set) 8 Cups - No Handles) 1 Teapot) No Saucers or Plates)	31.50
PL 130	8-Piece Place Setting) and Lined Wood Canteen Box)	99.99
LS 137	4-piece Leather Luggage Set	60.75
FB 160	Folding Field Binoculars	65.75
GB 166	Leather Gladstone Bag	40.50
TC 171	Digital Travel Clock) Full Featured Quartz) Slim, Modern Wallet Design)	10.60
BR 180	Bedside Radio and Clock	17.80
TS 185	Travel Desk Set	10.50

* Does not include handling and delivery charge

Key in the above exercise (filename GIFT) for 10-pitch print-out. Embolden the heading in spaced capitals and use the automatic underline feature for the words underlined. When you have completed this exercise, turn to page 74 and follow instructions for text editing.

For an explanation of blocked tabulation with single-line column headings and footnotes, see TYPING FIRST COURSE, 5/E, page 133.

FOOTNOTES

63. **Target Time: 20 minutes**
Type the following on A4 paper in double spacing. Margins: 12 pitch 22-82, 10 pitch 12-72.

OFFSET LITHOGRAPHY

This method of duplication has certain advantages if a thousand or more copies are required, or paper, of a document. trs.

NP. A master is prepared on a metal* plate. Ordinary typewritten material, photographs, drawings, etc, can be photocopied & transferred to the metal plates. wh can be stored & used many times. It is also possible to type, or write directly, on to a paper plate. The paper plate wl produce up to 2,000 good copies.

stet. This method of copying is speedy, ‡ & it is possible to use different coloured inks, & varying sizes of paper.

Run on. Offset litho machines are expensive to buy, but the paper & ink are not, so the cost per copy is relatively low.

---

* As many as 50,000 copies can be made from one master using a metal plate.

‡ Some offset litho machines can copy up to 17,000 pages per hour.

BLOCKED TABULATION WITH SINGLE-LINE COLUMN HEADINGS AND FOOTNOTES

69. **Target Time: 10 minutes**

Type the following exercise on A5 portrait paper. Centre vertically and horizontally in blocked style. Type in double spacing.

CALORIE CONTENT OF YOUR FAVOURITE CHEESE

Calorie intake may affect your weight

Cheese	Quantity	No of calories
Brie	2 oz*	180
Cheddar	2 oz	240
Cheshire	2 oz	220
Cottage	2 oz	60
Cream	2 oz	460
Danish Blue	2 oz	206
Edam	2 oz	180
Processed	2 oz	212
Stilton - white	2 oz	270

* 2 oz is equivalent to 56.69 g

70. **Target Time: 15 minutes**

Type the following exercise on A5 landscape paper. Centre vertically and horizontally in blocked style. Type in double spacing.

MOTOR CAR OPTIONAL EXTRAS

PART	LIST PRICE	CAR TAX	VAT	TOTAL
	£	£	£	£
Air Conditioning	903.04	75.25	146.74	1,125.03*
Electric Windows	173.67	14.47	28.22	216.36
Leather Trim	702.83	58.57	114.21	875.61
Headlamp Power Wash	133.74	11.15	21.73	166.62
Black Paint Finish	88.06	7.34	14.31	109.71

* Does not apply to coupé models

FOOTNOTES

64. **Target Time: 20 minutes**

Type the following on A4 paper in single spacing. Margins: 12 pitch 22-82, 10 pitch 12-72.

LAWRENCE OF ARABIA

Thomas Edward Lawrence* was born in North Wales on 16 Aug 1888. He was brought up in Oxford where he went to Jesus College & obtained a first-class honours degree in Modern History. [NP/] As a youth he preferred solitary pursuits, & he travelled over most of France alone. As a postgraduate he went to Syria, & later travelled across Egypt & Greece paying his way by doing odd jobs — camel driving & helping w the harvest.

He had many famous friends including Sir Winston Churchill, Thomas Hardy & Bernard Shaw.

In the 1914-1918 war he was a British military intelligence officer at British Headquarters in Cairo, & then he worked at the Arab Bureau. [Run on] Then followed his famous exploits for which he was to become known as Lawrence of Arabia, when he became leader of the Arab Revolt. He was awarded various decorations for his almost fanatical bravery, but he refused to accept them.

Lawrence of Arabia became a legend in his own short lifetime. He died as the result of a motor-cycle accident in Dorset at the age of 46.

---

* Author of 'Seven Pillars of Wisdom' & 'The Mint'.

Key in exercise 64 (filename ARAB) for 15-pitch print-out. Embolden the main heading. When you have completed this exercise, turn to page 74 and follow the instructions for text editing.

For an explanation of typing footnotes, see TYPING FIRST COURSE, 5/E, page 120.

CIRCULAR LETTERS

68.   **Target Time: 20 minutes**

Type the following circular letter on A4 plain paper. Use suitable margins. Turn up 10 single spaces so that the date and the name and address of the addressee may be inserted before a letter is sent out to an individual customer. Take a carbon copy.

Our Ref   PB/BD/BusEdu

Dear Sir/Madam

SECRETARIAL STUDIES by Betty Liddell

This text gives a realistic impression of the duties that a secretary is required to perform in a company. The book is divided into 12 sections, ea. of wh. looks at a diff. co. The student is given a job description & general informn. abt. the co. & is then asked to carry out various tasks. The teacher's manual provides the assignments & docs. for ea. task.

It has bn tried & tested in the classroom & forms an ideal way of bringing students into the real world of business.

THE PRACTICAL SECRETARY by Hones and Whitehead

(Typist - please take information fr. p. 76)

Yrs ffy

MARKETING
McGRAW-HILL BOOK COMPANY (UK) LIMITED

(TYPIST - please type name of co. where shown)

Key in the above document (filename BOOKS) for 10-pitch print-out. Embolden the titles of the books and justify the right margin. File document. When you have completed this exercise, turn to page 74 and follow instructions for text editing.

For an explanation of circular letters, see TYPING FIRST COURSE, 5/E, page 125.

ENUMERATIONS USING ROMAN NUMERALS

65. Target Time: 9 minutes

Type the following exercise on A5 landscape paper in double spacing. Margins: 12 pitch 22-82, 10 pitch 12-72.

E N G L I S H   U S A G E

The copy typist and the audio typist can be effective only if they can

I   spell and punctuate

II   apply common rules of grammar

III   use the apostrophe to show possession as in

      i   The man's golf bag had been lost.

      ii   The men's golf bags had been lost.

IV   form plurals and compound words

V   distinguish between the use of the hyphen and the dash.

66. Target Time: 8 minutes

Type the following exercise on A5 portrait paper in single spacing with double between the numbered items — the same style as the exercise above. Margins: 12 pitch 13-63, 10 pitch 6-56.

    QUALITIES AND QUALIFICATIONS

    <u>The Junior Typist</u>

    No doubt you are well aware that in order to be appointed as a Junior Typist, you must acquire certain qualifications and qualities.

    Your employer would prefer you to have

       I   an Elementary Certificate in
            i   Typewriting
            ii   Audio Transcription
            iii   Word Processing
       II   a good knowledge of English usage and modern business expressions
       III   a good knowledge of the basic principles of arithmetic
       IV   a willingness to work amicably with other people
       V   the ability to use resource and reference materials
       VI   a good telephone technique
       VII   a favourable disposition towards changing technology.

For an explanation of enumerations when using roman numerals, see TYPING FIRST COURSE, 5/E, page 124.

CIRCULAR LETTERS

67. Target Time: 20 minutes

Type the following circular letter on A4 headed paper (Kenkott Scotia PLC. Margins: 12 pitch 22-82, 10 pitch 17-72.

Our Ref MD/BD/CAR

Today's date

Dear Shareholder

I am pleased to have this opportunity to report to you about your company, & in th. way keep my promise th. I wd. inform you abt developments.

RESEARCH AND DEVELOPMENT

We have a £200 million annual research and development programme for supporting home industry, and over 94 per cent of our capital purchases comes from UK suppliers.

QUALITY OF SERVICE

There hv. bn. complaints, but our sights for the future are set much higher. As key elements in reaching a higher standard, we are investing in new machinery & equipment.

INVESTMENT

The co's. continued financial strength makes it possible for us to invest more than ever before, to improve the service we give to our customers & to secure the future prosperity of the co.

DIVIDEND

After allowing for taxation & dividend pd. on preference shares, earnings per ordinary share, at 10.4 pence per share, were 22% higher. I wl continue to keep you informed abt our progress.

Yrs ffy

Brian Davidson
Managing Director

Key in the above document (filename MAN) for 12-pitch print-out. Embolden the shoulder headings. File document. When you have completed this exercise, turn to page 74 and follow instructions for text editing.

For an explanation about the typing of circular letters, see TYPING FIRST COURSE, 5/E, page 125.